Praise for *The Passionate Mom*

"Every mother's goal is to see her child... *The Passionate Mom*, Susan Merri... ...men need to be successful moms, b... ...lan to help develop those qualitie... ... in the difficult task of raising chi...

—...ren and Tony Dungy

"Being a mother is the greatest joy of my life. My friend Susan Merrill regularly inspires me in my role as a mother. In her book, she will inspire you! *The Passionate Mom* is a book all mothers need to read. It will help each one become a better person and a better mother, no matter their children's ages. I encourage all passionate moms to take the lessons learned here, and use them to lovingly guide their children."

—Denise Jonas, mother of Kevin,
Joe, Nick, and Frankie Jonas

"If you are looking for encouragement as a mom as well as some very practical help in being a mom, you've found it in *The Passionate Mom*. As a skilled mom of five, Susan knows the exhausting challenges that encompass being a mom and has masterfully woven her story, along with the timeless truths of Scripture to equip you and give you hope."

—Dr. Dennis Rainey, host
of *FamilyLife Today*

"Susan Merrill has done her homework, and the result is a book that will be a vital guide for me for the next ten years, as I try to navigate my kids through grade school, middle school, and high school and launch them into life. This book reaches mothers like me at both the heart level and the head level, showing us how to guide our children passionately and practically. You can tell Susan knows firsthand what it is to love your children so much, yet still wonder how to parent them best. This is a book that will truly help me say what I long to be able to say one day: 'I'm not perfect, but I really did do my best.'"

—Shaunti Feldhahn, social
researcher, national speaker, and
best-selling author of *For Women Only*

"I have known Susan Merrill for many years, and I can tell you that she is the Passionate Mom! In this book, Susan shares her own stories as a mom—both her successes and challenges. You find yourself able to answer one of your most important questions, 'Am I a good mom?' With this handbook for mothering, you will have a plan in place and a road map in hand for passionately and confidently raising your child."

"Do you long to make every moment count? Want to be a purposeful mom? Do you desire to help your child succeed in this world? If your answer is yes to any of those questions, you need the words on these pages. Susan Merrill is a mom who gets it. She's honest, wise, experienced, and offers practical strategies to help you be the intentional mom you want to be."

"As I have journeyed and fumbled my way through motherhood, there are few seasoned moms I have met along the way that I would love to sit for hours over coffee to engage in honest, authentic dialogue about the struggle to do what it takes to be passionate, loving moms. Susan Merrill is one of those rare and real women. This book flows not just out of head knowledge, but out of the soul of real parenting from the real trenches of Susan's life. This is the kind of God-centered wisdom I cherish and seek—wisdom that digs deep and inspires me to stay the course and to see God's call on my life as a mom as sacred, focused, and set apart for the sake of my children."

The Passionate

Dare to Parent in Today's World

SUSAN MERRILL

THOMAS NELSON
Since 1798

NASHVILLE   DALLAS   MEXICO CITY   RIO DE JANEIRO

Published in Nashville, Tennessee, by Thomas Nelson. Thomas Nelson is a trademark of Thomas Nelson, Inc.

Thomas Nelson, Inc., titles may be purchased in bulk for educational, business, fund-raising, or sales promotional use. For information, please e-mail SpecialMarkets@ThomasNelson.com.

Library of Congress Cataloging-in-Publication Data

Merrill, Susan, 1962–
    The passionate mom : dare to parent in today's world / Susan Merrill.
    p. cm
Includes bibliographical references.
ISBN 978-1-59555-509-0
1. Mothers—Religious life. 2. Motherhood—Religious aspects—Christianity. I. Title.
    BV4529.18.M47 2013
    248.8'431—dc23   2012043387

Printed in the United States of America

13 14 15 16 17 18 RRD 6 5 4 3 2 1

For Megan, Emily, Hannah, Mark, and Grant—
you are my favorite open door.
I love you.

See, I have placed before you an open door that no
one can shut.
I know that you have little strength,
yet you have kept my word and have not denied my
name.

—Revelations 3:8

Contents

Introduction

Mom. Was there ever a job that encompassed so much, prompted so many questions, and created so many doubts in the minds of women?

What exactly is the job description for a mom? How can the job look so different from house to house, from culture to culture? Who is doing it *right*? Is there *one* right way, or *many*, depending on your child's personality, age, or environment? What if you have multiple children with diverse personalities? Should you parent them each differently under the same roof—is that even possible?

I am a mom to five children. I have girls and boys, biological and adopted, strong willed and compliant, creative and analytical, introverted and extroverted. The combinations of children and situations a mom can have are endless. Your child may be completely different from your sister's daughter or your friend's son, and therefore requires a different set of parenting skills. How do you know, with all the methods and advice, if you are parenting right? How can you be confident that you are being the best mom you can be for your children?

The question that most haunts me is, am I doing this right? At every stage of my children's development, doubts about my parenting abilities have popped up in various forms. These doubts are daunting. They can easily discourage, intimidate, and overwhelm me. And the questions! Things like:

- How long should I let her cry before I go in her room and pick her up for the fifth time tonight?
- When should I send her to school—and to *which* school?
- How do I teach character?
- What should the consequences be for lying, arguing, or disobeying?
- How much importance should I place on academics, sports, activities, and socializing?
- Do they really need to do all that to get into college?
- Am I *really* the only mom who won't let her kids see X, listen to Y, and have Z?
- Am I being firm enough? Am I being too harsh?
- Should I let her go? Is it safe?
- Is there something wrong with him? Is this normal?
- Are other moms worried about this? Or am I the only one? Who can I ask? Who can I trust?
- Am I doing this right?

Why isn't there a Google map for moms, or a handy iPhone app? Wouldn't it be amazing if you could input all the variables and characteristics of your children, press a button, and print the perfect parenting plan to follow? I have read lots of great parenting books and research, and I learned a great many things from them. But most address specifics, such as discipline or education or toddlers or teenagers. None gave me that overall vision that I wanted, the overarching plan that I needed.

And then one day I found it in an unusual place from an unusual source. I know it sounds crazy, but I found my parenting vision and plan in the Old Testament book of Nehemiah.

NEHEMIAH: AN UNLIKELY GUIDE

Stay with me, now.

Nehemiah was an amazing man who lived about twenty-five hundred years ago. Yes, the world has changed a bit since then, but let me tell you something: Nehemiah had a passion for the people he loved, just as we moms have a passion for the children we love.

Nehemiah was born into a time fraught with change and uncertainty. In 586 BC, the king of Babylon captured Nehemiah's people, the Israelites. The Babylonian army then ransacked, destroyed, and burned the city of Jerusalem, including Solomon's temple and the wall protecting the city. Those Israelites who survived were enslaved and marched eight hundred miles away, to Babylon.

Forty-seven years later the king of Persia invaded and conquered the Babylonians, and he encouraged the Israelites to return to Jerusalem; so they did. Once resettled there, they worked to restore what the Babylonians had destroyed.

After years of hard work, the poor Israelites managed to restore the temple, but that was as far as they got. The city and its surrounding wall were still a mess, and years passed by with the people and the temple exposed and in danger. The Israelites needed a leader to rebuild the wall and to provide protection and a future.

Nehemiah was the answer.

His mission was to build a wall around the city of his people for their safety and security. It was a seemingly insurmountable task, with impossible odds for any man. Most moms probably think the same thing—*this job of parenting is basically impossible for any woman.* But Nehemiah did not concern himself with impossibilities, and neither should we. His vision was bigger than the obstacles. He was called to build the wall to protect his people and provide them a secure future. Similarly, regardless of the challenges we face, we need to protect our kids and provide them a secure future.

Nehemiah had what every mother needs to parent well in today's world, and he provided a pattern for us to follow. That pattern is marked by ten Ps that we'll explore in the coming chapters:

1. Perception
2. Pondering
3. Passion
4. Prayer
5. Patience
6. Preparation
7. Purpose
8. Planning

9. Problem solving
10. Perseverance

Cultivating these ten Ps and learning how they fit together will help you accomplish your goal of being the best mom you can be.

We can see how they unfold in the life of Nehemiah. He knew what he was called to do. He *perceived* the situation, he *pondered* every task, he was driven with *passion* to search for solutions, he *prayed* for direction, he *patiently* waited for opportunities, he methodically *prepared* to take action, he maintained his *purpose*, he developed the *plan*, and he *persevered* through problems to the end.

Things did not always go the way Nehemiah would have liked, but no matter what happened, he performed well. He could not control the outcome, but he could control his own performance. And when it was all said and done, he could look back and say, "I did what I was called to do, and I did it well." That is all we can do as moms. So, where do we start?

Nehemiah loved his people, and he knew they needed a wall to protect them and provide them a future hope. We're not going to build literal walls, as Nehemiah did, but we can follow Nehemiah's basic insight. Our children need walls. That's why God gives them moms.

BUILDING THE WALL

As Nehemiah shows us, there are two dimensions to the wall you build for your child—protection and provision. The wall protects your child from exposure to harm from the outside world. The gates in the wall provide your child access to the training he or she needs to wisely navigate in the world, independent of you. You are the wall and the gates, the protection *from* the world and the provider of training for life *in* the world—and when you finish this book, you will have a plan to raise wise children who become independent adults with a promising future.

Protection

In the coming chapters we will learn from Nehemiah how to rebuild our concept of parenting—and ultimately ourselves as effective moms. Nehemiah used bricks and mortar, and so shall we. The "bricks" we will use to build our parenting are our ten Ps. To secure those bricks so that the wall is strong and effective, we need mortar. The mortar is our *character*, made up of the traits that moms must personally develop to effectively hold our bricks in place. These include, among other qualities, love, humility, discernment, determination, and self-control. We each will become a solid wall of nurturing protection for our children when these bricks are in place and we have become moms of character, adept at protecting our children. But once protection is considered, we need to focus on provision.

Provision

Nehemiah's wall had ten gates, and so will ours (we will discuss them later). The gates in the wall represent opportunities for your child to leave the protection offered by you—the wall—and explore the world. Many of these gates are common privileges, such as having a cell phone or driving a car. Some are seen as a rite of passage in our culture, based on a child's age. But age does not guarantee wisdom, and sometimes a mom needs to close a gate opened too soon. In this book we will discuss how a mom can provide her child a safe future by training the child in how to use these privileges, or gates. We will also examine how you can open and close the gates with wisdom so your child learns how to wisely operate in the world without risking his or her future. To do that, a mom must become a gatekeeper.

The first dimension of the wall is easy to understand. At birth your child was placed in your arms, and you encircled your innocent, defenseless infant with a protective embrace. You perceived your baby's every need. You pondered the purpose of every cry.

But babies grow. On top of physical needs, children develop more emotional and intellectual needs. They learn to walk, learn what makes them happy, learn to speak. Still, you keep them close; you're still the wall. You catch them when they fall, make them laugh when they cry, and patiently encourage them all along the way.

And they keep growing. Physically, they need you less, but emotionally and intellectually, they need you more. Spiritually too. But they may not realize it.

You let them out of your sight more and more. Emotionally, they begin to find happiness in friends and entertainment outside the home. They find intellectual satisfaction at school. You pitch in as needed—healthy meals and doctor visits, birthday parties and playdates, tutoring and school projects, church and Sunday school—but as your child grows, he or she seems to require you less than before, and your focus shifts away from being a wall.

The mortar weakens. The bricks get loose. The wall begins to break down. The gates are left open.

Your children look big and independent, but they are not. What wisdom can a child have at age ten, twelve, or even sixteen? They are still so young, so confidently foolish. They may need you less physically, but they need your provision for their emotional, intellectual, and spiritual health now more than ever.

────────────── **Confession** ──────────────

I did not believe that my children would need me more when they were older.

I have a very close group of seven friends. We call ourselves the "Beach Haven Babes" because we took our combined twenty children to the beach every summer. My children were the youngest, and for years as we regularly met for birthday lunches, I would soak up the wisdom of the more experienced moms as I listened to them talk about their older children. Often the discussion would lead to the children's activities, schedules, plans, and how busy, busy, busy they were, keeping it all afloat. On several occasions I clearly remember thinking in response to their chatter, *How can they be so busy? Their kids are in school from 8:00 to 3:00—that equates to eight free hours a day. My children are home all day, and when I am out, I am on the clock with a babysitter that I must pay and a nursing baby I must rush home to feed!*

xvi

For some reason I was under the impression that my children would need me more when they were younger, but I was wrong. My friends were really good, hands-on moms. My older children needed me just as much as, if not more than, they did at the age of two. The reality is that with every year that children age, there is more to do. The complexity and dimension of a child rapidly increases with years. Again, I am not an expert, but it seems to me that as children's physical growth slows, their complexity explodes. When my girls' growth slowed at about twelve, I noticed that I was increasingly challenged mentally as their emotional and social awareness expanded. With my boys, it was a few years later, at about age fourteen, that I had to step up my game.

The world is fraught with change and uncertainty today, just as it was in Nehemiah's world and probably has been in every age throughout history. No matter what the era, parenting children has always required the fortitude of a hearty pioneer. It still does. So whatever terrain your child leads you through, you must be willing to navigate it.

Do you feel as if your children have already been carried off into captivity? Or are you obliviously floating through life without really looking at where your children are headed? Are you afraid to make a mistake? Are you discouraged because you feel you have already made too many? How can we be sure we are navigating our children in the right direction?

So many questions. Believe me; I have asked them all.

Take comfort in this: there is nothing new under the sun. Do not allow yourself to fall into the trap of feeling alone in your struggles. And do not give up, thinking that parenting is harder today than ever before. It is changing and challenging, but life always is.

Wherever you find yourself and your family, if you're a passionate mom, not only do you have to be the wall; you also have to be the builder of the wall. You are Nehemiah to your child. Nehemiah wept with passion for his people. You will weep with the same passion over the danger to your child. Nehemiah's passion drove him to develop and execute a plan to better protect his people. You will take the time to develop a plan to protect and provide for your child. *Only* you. It is your calling, just as it was Nehemiah's. You are the one. And you can do it brick by brick.

And so we begin to build with the first of the ten Ps, the first of our bricks, *perception*.

1

Perception

> Those who survived the exile and are back in the province are in great trouble and disgrace. The wall of Jerusalem is broken down, and its gates have been burned with fire.
>
> —Nehemiah 1:3

Nehemiah was born in exile but possessed the enviable position of cupbearer to a powerful king. At first, this job seems menial and possibly dangerous. After all, the cupbearer's job was to ensure that the king's wine wasn't poisoned—by drinking it himself. But the cupbearer had important advantages, including constant access to the king. It was common for a cupbearer to acquire influence and intimacy with the king.

So what was Nehemiah thinking at this point in his life? I picture him as a man of good standing, content with his productivity and position, and probably not looking to make a move. But, of course, God is always on the move.

One day Nehemiah received a visit from his brother,

Hanani, and some friends. Nehemiah questioned his visitors, in search of news about their people who had survived the Babylonian exile and returned to Jerusalem. The news was not good: "Those who survived the exile and are back in the province are in great trouble and disgrace. The wall of Jerusalem is broken down, and its gates have been burned with fire" (Neh. 1:3).

And then the waitress brought Nehemiah and his guests some dessert, and they discussed their upcoming holiday and vacation plans.

I'm kidding. But isn't that the way it usually goes with visits from our friends? How many times have I sat having coffee with a friend or phoned my sister and discussed the news? We talk about the lives of others, but do we really care?

When you hear of a broken marriage, a rebellious teen, or a financial misfortune, do you respond with interest, concern, and caring, shaking your head sadly over the tragic news? And what about bad news from *your own* kids' lives? Do you give them your undivided attention and respond with genuine empathy? Or do you thank goodness that the waitress came around again and allowed you to change the topic?

Could this possibly be the way it goes with your after-school discussions with your child?

"Mom, I saw something really weird on the computer today."

"Mom, my friend is having a slumber party, but I don't like spending the night there."

"Mom, my teacher said I make my nines and sixes wrong."

"Mom, I saw a girl picking on Sissy in the lunch room."

And then you pull in the drive and tell the kids to grab

their stuff for ballet and baseball while you prepare a quick snack. Families are busy, and sometimes the providential hints about deeper issues get glossed over as we race through life.

Nehemiah did not gloss over what he heard from his brother. The city and the walls surrounding and protecting Nehemiah's people were a mess, but he did not move on to more pleasant topics. He listened. He *perceived*. The Bible says he questioned his visitors (Neh. 1:2). He assimilated and processed the information; he thought about what it meant to the safety and welfare of the people. He grieved their danger and their future.

The Israelites were in trouble, and what they needed was for someone to notice. They needed someone to rightly *perceive* the situation and take action. They had their man in Nehemiah. Do your children have their mom in you? Is there something going on in your child's life that she really needs you to perceive? Is she attempting to navigate some difficult waters without guidance because you haven't been listening?

Nehemiah had developed something every mom needs: depth perception. Perception is the vital ability to listen and process what is really happening in someone's life. It is not easy to force yourself to fully comprehend difficulties and to feel concern and even anguish, but for a mom it is necessary. So here is the first brick in building your own wall:

Brick #1
Perception
A Passionate Mom must perceive what is happening in her child's world.

My daughter Emily loved school until third grade. Then, out of the blue, she became increasingly distracted, grumpy, unorganized, and frustrated when she came home from school. Her grades were slipping. I jumped around a lot in my conclusions. Mostly, I blamed her. I thought she was goofing off because I had found lots of notes in her backpack that were being passed around in class.

The situation did not improve, and she was really getting frustrated with me getting frustrated with her. Then one day I learned that her teacher's health had been failing for months, and the teacher was leaving the class. Because the teacher didn't have the energy to teach, the class had gotten out of control. My daughter does not function well in chaos; she is easily distracted. The result was sketchy performance and irritability that were not her fault.

I had neglected to question her, listen to her, and assimilate the information I received. In other words, I had failed to perceive the situation and take appropriate action. Fortunately for my daughter, several other parents had better depth perception than I and had made the principal aware of the problem.

ALERTNESS, AVAILABILITY, AND ATTENTIVENESS

Nehemiah was miles away from his people when he heard the bad news, but he still cared about them and made it his business to know their world. He was *alert* to the cares of those he loved. Nehemiah was a very busy man, with a job that easily could have gone to his head and made him selfish, but it didn't. He was *available* to listen to his friends. Nehemiah put aside his busy concerns and inquired intently about the Israelites' welfare. He was *attentive*. Because Nehemiah was alert, available, and attentive, he got it. He fully understood the magnitude of the danger his people were in without a wall to protect them.

Children spend hours away from their moms—eight hours at school, two or three more hours in activities. They live a vast majority of their day in a world different from ours. How is your perception? Do you know this world well? Are you alert to the dangers present there? Are you available to talk when your kids are in the mood to share? Do you have an open rapport with them so you'll have the opportunity to hear about what transpires in their daily lives?

And what about others who live their lives in your children's world? Are you attentive to all who may be a source of information about your kids? Do you take opportunities to seek news from teachers, other parents, and coaches?

Alertness, availability, and attentiveness are traits that a mom *must* possess. They are necessary ingredients in the mortar that will hold the brick of perception in the wall.

Alertness: a keen awareness of what takes place around you that enables you to respond correctly to it

When my nephew and niece were just two and four, my sister, Kathie, started using a new babysitter. The sitter was highly recommended, and Kathie was thankful to have a regular sitter for Saturday nights.

Neither of the children had ever fussed when my sister and brother-in-law left them with previous sitters, but after just one occasion with the new sitter, four-year-old Maggie, who is normally very independent and outgoing, became shy and clingy when the sitter arrived. By the third Saturday night, Kathie had a feeling something was not right. There were subtle changes in my niece's personality and sleeping habits. There weren't any bruises or other signs of mistreatment, and the kids responded well to the sitter when they saw her in public, but Kathie's "Mommy senses" were on alert. Her husband told her she was being paranoid and attributed the changes to a "mommy phase," but Kathie could not let it go and set up a hidden video camera.

The video explained everything. The sitter and the children watched television the entire night—graphic, crime-solving TV shows that were frighteningly inappropriate for a two- and a four-year-old. The video also showed the sitter having dinner, but she never fed the children. Instead, she put them to bed and ignored their cries. Needless to say, this sitter never returned, and my sister learned to stay alert to those subtle changes in her children's personalities.

Availability: a willingness to make your schedule secondary to the needs of your children

Do you have a chatty child? I have some who chat and some who don't. The former require that you make yourself available for hours. For every five thousand words they speak, there will be those fifty that you really need to hear—but you only hear them if you make yourself available to listen. Some time ago my most romantic child wrote this about the countless hours she needed my availability:

Then there is the subject of L.O.V.E. Love can mean so many different things. But young love can be confusing. I, unfortunately, am the kind who falls in and out of "love" as fast as you take on and off your shoes. I like to think I'm a lover, not a liker. I couldn't begin to count the times I cried to my mother, swearing that this guy was the one of my dreams! I realize it could have gotten a tad bit annoying, but one thing I am so grateful to my mother for was her patience. She gave me her time and allowed me to grieve. After all, it is a tough world out there—especially for impressionable girls like me. We meet a boy, then like the boy, then—*whoa*—we suddenly love the boy! It just happens—we can't help it. Unfortunately, it most often doesn't work out the way we want, and our heart gets broken. My mother gave me the best gift when this happened to me. She let me grieve. She let me have feelings and let me express them to her. She didn't scold me and tell me to get over it! No, she just held me and explained, "Honey, it happens . . . I had to wait a long time until I found your daddy. And when I finally did find him, I had to wait a lot longer until we were together." Love takes patience, and I thank God that my mom was patiently there for me.

A lot of little children just babble about their days, and most multitasking moms can listen while still executing a few little tasks. It can become a dangerous habit, though, and may result in you tuning out your children. Nancy, a friend and coworker, is wonderful about putting everything else aside and listening to her children (and me) because she values people. She has made it a commitment to

Attentiveness: an eagerness to show one's worth to you by giving your undivided attention to that individual's words

The Passionate MOM

sit down with her children at the table after school during their snack to fully participate in conversation that usually evolves into a length of time because she is engaged.

For me, attentiveness means staying up until my children come home—following them into their rooms and hanging up clothes as they change and brush their teeth. It may sound as though I am catering to my children, but having small tasks to do is a natural reason for me to be with them, and they will often open up and chat about the night while I'm helping out.

TWO KINDS OF PERCEPTION

Perception can be both offensive and defensive. Let me explain.

Offensive Perception

Sometimes perception can be used *offensively* to help us encourage our children. For example, you may perceive through observation that your child has a gift. Offensive perception can further help you assimilate information about that child's abilities and giftedness and how best to foster them.

When our first two children were very young, they went to a wonderful, very structured school. Our firstborn, Megan, fit right into the structure and did very well. We loved the program.

Two years later Emily started school there too. After her fourth day, she jumped into the car and announced that she had been sent "to the wall." The wall is where you had to stand if you were in trouble. Megan had never been sent to the wall in two years, but Emily was sent there after just four days. I was alarmed.

"Why were you sent to the wall?" I asked.

"Ariel Mermaid was playing in my head, and I just had to sing her out," she proudly exclaimed.

One week later Emily informed me—a bit more hesitantly because she now knew that I would not be excited about her announcement—that she had been sent to the wall again. Yikes. "Why?" I asked.

"I ate some Play-Doh," she sheepishly answered.

I reminded her that we had already explored Play-Doh and that it was not flavored; every color tasted the same.

"But, Mommy," she said, "it was a *new color*, and I wanted to be sure."

I made an "offensive perception" about Emily at that point. Based on her first few weeks at school, I perceived that this child had a creative bent, and I had better find an outlet for it so she could control her creativity in school! Offensive perception can give a mom vision about her child and help her *take action* to encourage that child in his or her area of giftedness.

Defensive Perception

Other times perception can be used *defensively* to protect our children. You may perceive that your child is making unwise choices and getting into trouble. Defensive perception can help you protect and redirect that child. This is particularly true during the middle school and high school years. These are times of extreme flux for a child, and you never know exactly what may happen.

One of our children spent the first twelve years of life in an impoverished country. When we adopted her, she had a hard time with food. Its abundance and availability were a distraction for her and invoked the early signs of a potential eating disorder.

She started her education here in a tiny private school where everyone brought his lunch and there were only five children in her grade. The school was the perfect fit for her, and because she was extremely bright, she quickly caught up to her grade level. Then she moved to a much larger middle school.

It was a big jump, but not academically. She was up for the challenge in that category. What overwhelmed her was going from the lone picnic table at her little school to what equated to a food court at her new school. There were too many choices of food to buy, and too many people to share food with or receive leftovers from.

As we chatted during the first few weeks, I focused on her social adjustment because the school was much bigger, and I was concerned about her adjusting to life there. She had a new friend whom I asked about often. The girl was quite small and shy, but so was my daughter, so I thought they might forge a unique and empathetic bond. But from bits of conversation here and there, I learned that the new friend was very thin and was required by her teachers to leave class to eat snacks at certain times. She had a disorder, and I was troubled to realize that my daughter was enjoying far too much of the food that her friend desperately needed to eat but didn't want.

I made a "defensive perception" about my daughter. She was tempted by food and was not, at that point, able to withstand the temptation. Her friendship was not healthy for her or for her friend. She was happily overeating food that was meant for a child who needed to eat it. Defensive perception helps us see situations that require action to protect our children from temptations that they are not mature enough to handle and to train them in ways to overcome weaknesses.

These two forms of perception work together. When we

adopted our son, he was already nine years old. Grant had lived in a village in Siberia, where he had never gone to school and pretty much had always done what he wanted, when he wanted. This meant that he was used to bouncing around like a Ping-Pong ball at every hour of the day *and* night.

The overactive Grant hit the limit at about month three into the adoption. It was Christmas break. All the kids were home all day. In Florida, that means playing outside. Grant was out of control, and my kids weren't the only ones complaining. He was driving the neighborhood kids crazy. He was so out of control that he hit our neighbor in the face with a broom. The neighbor was a high school football player three times Grant's size. When the mother of a defensive lineman politely mentions to you that your son is being rough, you can't help perceiving you have a serious problem.

My defensive perception: Grant had a problem with self-control that stemmed from too much energy. So I had Grant get out my bike; then I hopped on and pedaled away. "Come with me," I yelled over my shoulder.

He happily ran after me, and we continued for about half a mile before he said (and I wish you could have heard it in his little Russian accent), "Mom, what are we doing?"

I explained that from that day forward he had to run around the block whenever he did something wrong. I then told him that he had seven blocks to run for the seven misdemeanors so far that day.

"Okay," he said, "what is this block for?"

"This block is for knocking your sister over."

And around and around we went. He chattered for 3.5 miles. He hopped on and off the curb, leapt over puddles, and jumped to swat tree branches. He wasn't even remotely out of breath. He was only nine. After that he usually had to run almost every day.

Months later I had an offensive perception: I could use Grant's energy problem as an opportunity. It was a week before the Gasparilla 15K, an annual nine-mile race in Tampa. I asked a friend of ours who was running in the race if he would let Grant pace behind him. He was fascinated with Grant's story and agreed.

At mile eight in the race, my friend, amazed that Grant did not even seem winded, cut him loose. He pointed to the finish line ahead and said, "Run, Grant, run!" Grant bolted for the entire remaining mile and won the race for his age group.

To this day Grant is still running, but not as a consequence for disobedience. He is running for pleasure in high school and winning at state competitions.

I perceived that Grant had a problem behaving because he had too much energy. Defensively, I had to do something to help him so he wouldn't get in trouble or fail in life. So I required him to run. Then I perceived that Grant was good at it and that his problem could be used offensively as an opportunity. I had to help him use his gift of unlimited energy to succeed.

THREE WAYS TO BE UNPERCEPTIVE

There are at least three ways to miss what's going on in your child's life:

1. Maintain a Stunted Perception

Developing perception is a choice, and some parents choose not to have it. Ignorance is bliss—for a time. Sometimes parents would rather not know what their child is doing. They just hope it will all work out. But this sort of stunted perception may end up hurting their child and other children. Kids know which parents care enough to perceive what they are doing and which parents don't, and they can identify the houses where it is safe to cross the line.

This came as a total surprise for me. My easiest child became more challenging as a teenager, and I was required to develop sonar with a depth perception radius of twenty miles. I never dreamed I had it in me. My child wasn't alone in his misadventures, and so, having learned the importance of the parenting network, I reached out to other parents to assimilate more information. I was very surprised to learn in the process that some of the parents had stunted perception. They really didn't want to know what was going on and chose to ignore their children's dangerous pursuits.

2. Practice Selective Perception

Sometimes parents can have selective sonar. These moms and dads can see a bad grade coming ten days into a new semester but never see a substance abuse problem until there is an arrest. They have their area of concern but are willing to let other areas slide. It takes a tough mom to hold the line on all fronts.

Kids can really push back if they feel you won't let them do "anything." I know. I have shed many a private tear over hurtful, angry words from a frustrated teenager. For every time I heard, "You are the only mom who cares about this stuff," I had to tell myself a dozen times that there had to be other moms who care. I just couldn't always find them.

3. Apply a Politically Correct Perception

Some moms are perceptive and know what is going on but refrain from taking action because they believe it is politically incorrect. This is a painful delusion that can leave you paralyzed with fear. These moms are adept at assimilating information, but once they've attained it, they feel guilty because they have invaded their children's privacy. To know and not act is quite worrisome and torturous.

The politically correct mom also struggles with giving consequences. She knows what is going on and wants to take action, but consequences seem so cruel and, again, so politically incorrect. *How will my child survive if I take her cell phone away? Will he be permanently damaged if I take away the privilege of going to prom? playing in a game? going on a trip with friends? Will her boyfriend dump her if she can't go to the homecoming dance? Will the coach kick him off the team if I don't let him play in a game? Will her friends exclude her if I don't let her go on the trip? What if my kids hate me? Will they hate me if I give them a consequence?*

For a time, probably. But to learn from mistakes, they need to be held accountable for their actions, and you are the wall responsible for providing that accountability.

FOUR WAYS TO ADD DEPTH
TO YOUR PERCEPTION

Perceiving is the first thing Nehemiah did in his step toward building the wall, and it is the first brick in building our walls. How can we be more perceptive? How can we add depth to our perception? Here are four ways:

1. Think

How often do we hear or see things that we really don't think about. This is so easy to do with the distractions of our culture. I have been guilty of being so engrossed in my computer that I did not even look up when my daughter came home, tears running down her face as she ran up the stairs. I missed a huge opportunity to discuss deeply hurt feelings from the heart of my child. I was not thinking.

2. Engage

Nehemiah questioned his men. And we should question our kids. This does not mean interrogate, but it does mean that every day we should take an interest in our children's lives. It is the only way to really know what is going on in their hearts and minds. The earlier you start questioning, the more accepted and natural your questions will be to your children. If you wait till they are older to start engaging, they may be a little guarded. But it is never too late. Just start floating questions out there:

"Who do you like to eat lunch with?"

"Which of your friends is the funniest?"

"Who is the kindest?"

"If you had to go to work today, what would you want to do?"

"What is the biggest mistake you ever saw someone make?"

Then try to catch an answer. Sometimes you will not get one. I have heard "I don't know" hundreds of times. Just keep floating questions and developing the best approach for each child. iMOM has hundreds of free printable TALK cards with questions on every topic. Cut them up; put them beside your child's bed (they don't really want to go to sleep, so they will talk to put it off) or in a jar on the dinner table and make it a tradition to talk. See Resources page 231.

3. Listen

It really helps to remember that you are listening with the purpose of trying to understand your child. Your listening should be processing but not necessarily forming a response for your child. I am not very good at just listening without processing solutions.

I became acutely aware of this from Emily, my most expressive and affectionate child. Emily likes to express every emotion and drama of the day. Of course, I like to respond with lots of instruction about how she should have handled the situation and what the outcome could have been had she followed my instructions.

This scenario was playing out quite a bit in her sixth-grade year due to some girl drama with her little group of friends. Finally, after about three such situations in one week, she covered my mouth, midsentence, with her hand, burst into tears, and said, "Mom, please stop telling me what to do. I just want you to listen and hold me!"

4. Wait

If you offer solutions without waiting patiently to see what else may be forthcoming, you can miss out on really good information that may change your ideas. A child, especially an older one, may shut down if you start offering your opinion without all the facts. We will see that Nehemiah was a calculatedly patient man.

In my experience you have to wait more often with boys

than with girls. My girls are never worn out from my questions and delight in explaining every detail of their day. With the boys I have to be much more strategic. I have to gauge where they are that day on the "chatometer." Then if they run out of words, I just have to be quiet and patiently wait for another opportunity.

THE MOMMY MAFIA

Nehemiah had friends. Do you? Nehemiah's brother, Hanani, and some men went to visit him. They shared some precious news that he wanted to hear: their people were in trouble. Hanani and his friends were Nehemiah's eyes and ears for him. He was a busy man and couldn't be where he could see what he needed to see. Are your friends eyes and ears for you? You are a busy mom and can't be everywhere to see what you need to see.

Sharing information with friends about their children can be a rather tough thing for a mom. Many moms do not want to hear that their children are in trouble—remember that selectively perceptive type? With five teenagers, I have been on both sides of bad news, the giving and the receiving.

I say the following with great urgency and concern: ladies, swallow your pride and *listen.*

I try to have honest friendships with the parents of my children's friends. If I do not know them well, I will go to them and tell them that I value their child's relationship with mine. I ask them to be my eyes and ears, to share with me any information about my child that they think I need to know. And then I promise them that I will listen and receive what they have to say.

If you do this, you will quickly learn who is humbly open

17

to wanting to parent through the best and the worst. The surprising thing is that you will learn that there are parents who really don't want to know. They may deny what you tell them and walk away closed and sometimes even angry.

Moms, do not be one of them. If you are, you may close a door to future information that you need to know—information that could save your child from a troublesome situation, such as an abusive boyfriend or drugs. I know moms like this; they choose privacy and pride when what their children need is open and honest communication between parents that will deliver to them the protection of accountability.

Instead, try to build a group of moms who stand together; at iMOM we jokingly call this the "Mom Mafia." Here are some tips on starting your own Mom Mafia.

1. *Build relationships with key informants.*

   If you don't have a social relationship or friendship with any of the parents of your kids' friends, get busy. It's important to know these people well if your child is going to be hanging out in their homes and spending lots of time with their children. Find out if they share your values and have similar boundaries for their kids.

2. *Get over the guilt.*

   Some moms have been tricked into believing that to check up on their kids is to deny them respect and trust. But I promise you, the child who will kick and scream about this "invasion of privacy" may be the child who has something to hide. Your first job is to be a parent—not a friend.

3. Protect your sources.

    This one is from Intelligence Gathering 101. If another member of the Mom Mafia tells you that your seventh grader was sitting with a boy at the movies when you thought she was seeing the show with her girlfriends, *do not say*, "Mrs. Williams saw you and called me." That will only ensure that your child will hide her disobedience from Mrs. Williams as she hides it from you, making this informant ineffective in the future. Just let her wonder how you know—it will make her think the walls have eyes, and if that's what it takes to keep her honest, so be it.

4. Share and share alike.

    If you want other moms to go out on a limb for you, you need to be willing to do the same for them. Take the time to listen in when the gang is at your house for things that you know would be concerning to other moms, and use wisdom about when to "file a report." When in doubt, go ahead and share what you know, with the disclaimer that you don't know for sure if it is an issue, but you want the other mom to make that call.

5. Don't be overly sensitive.

    As moms, we're naturally protective of our children and want to defend them. So having another mom come to you and tell you that your child was seen drinking, or cheating on a test, or had some other breakdown in character or integrity can be hard. *Don't shoot the messenger,* as they say, *just because you don't like hearing the message.* Even if you think the other mom may have her information wrong in some way, thank her for caring about your child and being willing to intervene. If you make her feel like the villain, she'll never share again.

———

Do you have friends like Hanani who are brave enough and care enough about your child to share troublesome news with you? Are you humble enough to listen, or do you pretend they are wrong?

THE PASSIONATE MOM MUST PERCEIVE

Passionate moms are really perceptive moms. They don't just listen and move on. They try to understand what is *really* going on. Children today spend a lot of time away from their parents, in school and with friends, and their communication with friends is usually hidden in electronic devices. A mom following Nehemiah's pattern is alert, available, and attentive to her son or daughter so she can understand that child and the world in which he or she moves.

The Brick	The Mortar
Perception	Alertness
	Availability
	Attentiveness

Pondering

When I heard these things, I sat down and wept.
For some days I mourned and fasted . . .

—Nehemiah 1:4

Nehemiah was perceptive, so he pondered his people's desperate situation *for some days,* and he was so committed to his reflection that he fasted! Perception, the first brick in the wall, is the ability to see what is happening in your child's life. Pondering is deliberately contemplating the significance of what you perceive. *Pondering* is the next brick in our wall.

> *Brick #2*
> *Pondering*
> A Passionate Mom must carefully ponder her child and the significance of what is happening in that child's life.

Certainly Nehemiah was in a similar or even busier state than I am. He did not climb to the position of cupbearer to the king by slacking off and calling in sick. I imagine there was a healthy list of people waiting to step in and take his position if he had. There was a lot of pressure to keep up his performance at all times, and he probably had an endless "to do" list, but it did not distract him from the concern of the moment. His job was not going to usurp the importance of his people's needs. He knew his priority was to carefully ponder the devastation his people faced. Their lives and their future were at risk.

So Nehemiah, man of wisdom that he was, perceived the tragedy of the situation, and it grieved him. In fact, it grieved him so much that he took the time to mourn, fast, and pray about it *for days*. He allowed himself to feel the sadness of the situation. Painful, yes, but necessary if one is going to ponder something difficult. Nehemiah knew that Israel's plight was critical and that it had been brought to his attention for a reason, so he gave time for pondering his people's need.

Isn't that what we want to do for our children—deeply ponder what they need in life? How would our kids benefit if we made the time to really think about their character, their behavior, their struggles, strengths, and weaknesses? What if we purposed to dwell on things that, deep down, caused us to wonder from time to time? Could it help turn a child from destructive behavior? Could it even save a life? Might we discover a hidden talent or gift?

We used to call one of my daughters Snow White. She had such different coloring from her siblings, and it bothered her.

We live in Florida and love to be out on the water. Her brothers and sisters were of the easy-tanning sort, whereas our lovely little Snow White had to be slathered with sunscreen every four hours to avoid a severe blistering. She was never able to acquire that Florida tan.

The spring of her junior year of high school, after several trips to the lake, she excitedly informed me that she had a tan. Strangely enough, she did. And for several more months, every time she sat in my lap, I couldn't help noticing how brown her hands were. It bothered me. My husband thought it was nothing; my friend thought it was nothing; my daughter thought it was great.

Somewhere in the back of my mind, I remembered reading about skin developing more pigment. I started Googling and read about Addison's disease, but it was very rare. I finally took her to see the doctor. He wasn't too concerned and told me that he had never even seen a case in all his years of practice. But he ordered bloodwork.

Two days later I got an urgent call; my daughter was in danger and needed to see an endocrinologist immediately. She had Addison's disease.

Addison's is adrenal gland failure and is seldom diagnosed before there is an acute, life-threatening adrenal crisis because there are so few symptoms. The first question the endocrinologist asked me was, "How did you know?" I told her the Lord prompted me to notice, and when I did, he wouldn't allow me to let it go. I couldn't stop thinking about it. That doctor told me that my "pondering" may have saved my daughter's life.

IF YOU DON'T PONDER, WHO WILL?

"But Mary treasured up all these things and pondered them in her heart."

—Luke 2:19

What was Mary, the mother of Christ, pondering in this verse? Why had the Lord prompted her to ponder those things? Scripture doesn't say that anyone else was pondering, just Mary. How was she to make future use of the conclusions from her musing? I don't know how Mary put them to use, but I do know two things:

- Mary was chosen to be the mother of God's only Son; therefore, she is an excellent role model for me.
- Mary pondered those things that concerned her child; therefore, I should ponder things that concern mine.

Mothers have a gift of insight that is unique to them, and to protect our children, we must use it. I do not like to think about what would have happened to my daughter had the Lord not prompted me to ponder her beautiful new tan. Without perception and pondering as bricks in your wall, it may very well be impossible to protect your children and provide a future for them. I could have lost Emily. I could have failed to protect my daughter, and it may have cost her her future.

DOES ANYBODY REALLY HAVE
TIME TO PONDER?

It seems that no one today has *time* to ponder. We pack more into a day than ever before in history. But the reality is that we do still have time. Whenever I pitch the complaint to my husband that I just don't have the time to do something, he swats it right back with, "Everyone has time, and so do you. You are just not making this a priority for your time." Ouch. The point is, we do have time to ponder; we just use that time for other things. Pondering takes time, sometimes lots of it.

Shortly after we adopted our son, Grant, he did something that deeply grieved me. I didn't know all the details, but I knew he had done it. The magnitude of it was not surprising because he had been very neglected his first nine years of life. He had never gone to school or ridden in a car, and he didn't know the days of the week, the seasons of the year, or even his own birthday. He was, as I call him, our "Jungle Book boy" because he had pretty much raised himself in the woods of Siberia until he was found and put in an orphanage a year before we got him. So what he did, though not necessarily unpredictable, was dangerous, and needed to be addressed. I knew that he wasn't ready to receive correction about what had happened because he was frustrated and confused about his new life here. So I had to just ponder what to do and when to do it.

What happened stayed with me for months, and I continued to ponder and pray. After a time, his English improved, and he could even read a little. We started a journal to record events in his life because he had no prior record, not one baby picture. I decided that this action needed to go in his journal so he would remember it and never do it again. The problem was, he didn't know that I knew. If I confronted him with it, he was stubborn enough to deny it to his grave because he knew how much it would hurt me. So I needed him to confess on his own rather than try to force a confession. If I forced it, unlike a true confession of repentance, he might not grieve over it himself. He would just get angry and probably fall prey to the temptation to do it again. Once more, I pondered and prayed.

Then one day I decided it was time to go fishing for a confession. I figured my idea was vague enough that if he wasn't ready to face the misdemeanor, we would just wait and I would trust that God would make it clear in his time. So I wrote this in his journal:

> *I know that one day you will tell me about the _____.*
> *It will be a good day, and you will feel better.*

Of course, I filled in the blank in the journal, but for privacy I am leaving it blank for you. I had never said what I knew about what he had done, and he thought I had never even noticed anything. He immediately asked a lot of questions, like what did this mean, what did I know about it, and why would he feel better? I told him I wasn't quite sure, but that when I prayed about him, this is what I thought about.

Day after day he started dancing closer and closer to the truth. He was testing me to see what I knew by my reaction to his questions. For weeks as he danced, I pondered and prayed, until one day he danced so close that he broke down and cried and confessed. It was a true confession of repentance, and well worth the wait. We entered the lesson he had learned in his journal, and I am so thankful that he has never repeated the offense.

—————————— **Confession** ——————————

For every time I have perceived a lesson that my children needed to learn and pondered how to train them about it, I have probably missed three other lessons that they needed to learn. I wish I had pondered more.

Making time for pondering—for deliberately contemplating what you have perceived—is crucial to preparing a child for the future. We won't know how to train up a child if we haven't pondered what he needs training in.

CONTROLLING THE THINGS THAT KILL A COMMITMENT TO PONDER

So is pondering a thing of the past? Have we killed it?

I have a daughter majoring in musical theater. We have spent hours and hours watching old movies, and British films in particular. What always amazes me in period movies is how much time people of bygone days spent visiting, talking, walking, and just sitting. Without television and sports, there was not much entertainment other than philosophical conversation, books, and therapeutic walks, reflecting on life and nature.

We have so much more to entertain us today, and we may be giving our time to ponder the squeeze because of it. There are lots of fascinating distractions that are killing my pondering time. Maybe you can identify with me. I have thought on this a bit and found that I can narrow them down to two problems, with two solutions to remedy them.

Problem 1: Compulsiveness

This is the one that most severely affects me. Please note that all of life's distractions can be rationalized as worthy of my attention. After all, I am keeping up with friends and finding answers, even saving money. These are worthy endeavors—*sometimes*. But at other times they only distract me from what I should be doing—pondering. For example . . .

- *The phone.* I chat with friends endlessly, especially in the car, when I could just ponder each of my children while I drive.
- *The computer.* I shop online because I get way too many e-mails about great sales, and research online because Google has the answer to all my questions. (Of course, Google was important when I was researching my daughter's symptoms, but it is a distraction if I am Googling for hours without a commendable reason.)
- *Social media.* I use Facebook, Twitter, and Pinterest because it is so fun to celebrate and comment on my friends' pictures and posts.
- *Volunteer overcommitment.* I want to "be there," involved with every child and all their activities. But multiple children means multiple opportunities to volunteer, and it's so hard to say no.

Solution: Self-Control

I like to hop around in my thoughts and actions. Writing this book has been an enormous act of concentrated focus for me. I would much prefer to hop into doing one thing for twenty minutes, then hop on to my computer for twenty minutes, then fold one load of laundry, and so on throughout the day. Madison, who manages all the details I am not attentive to at iMOM (where I work), has a terrible time with me, poor thing. She has appointed herself my "wrangler," and I am sure she often regrets the job. I do not regret her at all and am very thankful that she wrangles me into finishing things and will not allow me to hop. The sad reality is she is almost half my age—I should have the self-control to wrangle myself!

The only way to fight distraction is with self-control.

———————— **Confession** ————————

I am *not* good at exercising self-control. I always have a perfectly rational excuse for what I am doing. And I am hardworking, so it is okay as long as I can justify it. Humph! I frustrate myself. Have you heard the phrase "I do what I don't want to do, and I don't do what I want to do"? That is me in a nutshell, and it is very discouraging. The only comfort I have is that I am not alone. It has been a problem throughout history. Paul the apostle, writing nearly two thousand years ago, confessed the very same thing! He said, "I do not understand what I do. For what I want to do I do not do, but what I hate I do" (Rom. 7:15).

Do you find comfort in knowing that there is nothing new under the sun? The same things you struggle with, others have struggled with—forever. We just have to keep fighting to develop our character. So here is something to put in the mortar of your wall to hold the brick of pondering in place. But know that it is a gritty one to mix in!

> **Self-control:** the ability to control your own behavior, especially in the face of compulsive distractions

Problem 2: Selfishness

The distractions I listed earlier can be selfish too, but I see a little difference in myself between the compulsiveness, which is not intentional, and selfishness, which I find very intentional. Often, the above distractions are not premeditated. The ones that follow usually become problematic because I have selfishly told myself that they're necessary or that I deserve them. Please do not misinterpret me. I am *not* saying a mom should not do any of these things—every mom needs a break. However, if the mode of entertainment or preoccupation is filling your calendar so that you don't have a minute to ponder, then the diversion has entered the danger zone.

- *Competitive leisure sports.* Participating in leagues that are ambitious can create pressure to spend more than the average amount of time playing.
- *Working out.* Fitness demands that we exercise for hours each week but not hours each day. Hours spent exercising every day may be an indicator that we have become slaves to vanity.

- *Television.* So many channels, so many series, we are easily enticed and entertained to the point that we can't miss an episode.
- *Work.* The bills must be paid, but sometimes we work more than we need to because we like it, it builds our sense of accomplishment, or we covet stuff and desire money to spend.
- *Shopping.* We all want to look as best we can, but looking fashionable takes time and effort whether we are on a budget or not.
- *Socializing.* Parties, clubs, Bunko, and bridge. Birthday lunches, work dinners, old friends and new. The socialite has a lot to keep up with and do.

Solution: Selflessness

The job of motherhood is a selfless one, to be sure. Moms do not get days off unless they have a substitute, and substitutes are hard to come by and costly. There will always be diapers to change, lunches to pack, laundry to wash, boo-boos to bandage, and little ones with fevers who need to be rocked. These are all basic needs that mothers meet. But as children grow, basic needs diminish. Diapers go away. Children can pack their own lunches and bandage their own boo-boos. What replace basic needs are more complicated emotional and relational needs. A child can live without us meeting those emotional and relational needs, but that doesn't mean they are unimportant.

Pondering takes selflessness. Selflessness is sacrificing what I want to do so I can do something for others. It means putting my children first. I can feel the quills spiking in some of you as I write this. Please understand: I know how hard you

Selflessness: the ability to put the needs and desires of others before your own

work as a mom, and I am so thankful that you do. I have five children, and there have been so many times that I only got about five or six hours of sleep a night for months on end—I thought I would never catch a break. But looking back, there are so many compulsive and selfish things that distracted me and ate up a lot of time that I could have put to better use.

Into the mortar we must throw *a lot* of selflessness.

EVERYBODY BENEFITS FROM SELF-CONTROL

Pondering takes selflessness, and selflessness takes self-control. It takes self-control to put down a good book when a child comes in bored and wants to play a game. It takes self-control to look up from Pinterest when your son walks in the door from school, or to get off the phone when your daughter needs help with homework. And it takes self-control to give up a party to help one of your kids with a school project or to cancel a tennis match to comfort a daughter who didn't get asked to the prom. It takes self-control to be *selfless*.

The great benefit of learning to exercise self-control is this: if you learn self-control, you will be better able to model it to your child. Self-control has another name: deferred gratification. The ability to exercise deferred gratification has been studied and is associated with success later in life. The best demonstration of this that I have seen is Stanford University's marshmallow experiment conducted in 1972.

The study was conducted on more than six hundred children, ages four to six. Each child was led into a room, empty of distractions, where a marshmallow was placed on a table. The children were each told they could eat the marshmallow, but if they waited for fifteen minutes to eat it, they would be rewarded with a second marshmallow.

There have been more recent marshmallow experiments where researchers have videotaped the children and posted the videos on YouTube. In the videos it is amusing to watch the children fight the temptation to eat the marshmallow. Some cover their eyes with their hands or turn around so they can't see it. Others start kicking the desk or playing with their hair. Some go so far as to smell the marshmallow and even lick it, while others simply eat the marshmallow as soon as the researcher leaves the room.

One-third of the children in the original experiment were able to resist the temptation to eat the marshmallow. The scientists then followed the children to see whether or not doing so had been a predictor of their future success. The children who were able to defer gratification and exercise self-control were significantly more competent, had higher SAT scores, and as of 2011 (the participants were around forty), the characteristic of self-control had remained with them for life.

There is an important lesson here for you and your child. It may be more important to teach your preschooler self-control than the ABCs and 123s. And if you, like me, lack self-control, researchers say it is never too late to learn. So go buy yourself some marshmallows or a bag of dark chocolate peanut M&M's and start practicing self-control!

THE PASSIONATE MOM MUST PONDER

A passionate mom must ponder everything she learns about her child so she can truly *know* her child. Do you add the bits of news and clues about your child's life like puzzle pieces to your understanding so you can assemble a clear picture of what is going on in his or her life?

One of my children is extremely quiet. One day, during his first quarter in high school, he randomly mumbled that his life would be much easier if he were a geek. I stopped dead in my tracks and pondered for a moment. I had been waiting for a sign like this—a clue as to how he was acclimating to and processing his new environment. You see, my son had moved from a small private school to a large public high school. I knew he was going to have to navigate new social waters in a much bigger pond. What he was really saying was, "I am feeling pressure to try to be something that is hard for me." He had observed that it might be easier if he were in a different crowd. He was struggling.

The vast majority of people are struggling with something on any given day, but most of us keep it to ourselves. Our children are no different. Have you perceived what your child is struggling with? Have you pondered it and carefully considered what course of action you should take to help? If not, are you exercising selflessness and self-control to ensure that you *take the time* to ponder so you can take the appropriate action?

We have learned so much from the intuitive Nehemiah already, and we have two bricks to show for it: we know how to perceive, and we know the importance of pondering. Next we will get to what drives the heart of this man and every mom—the fuel and fire that expand our capacity far beyond ourselves. We will learn that *passion* is the brick that can turn a wimpy wall into a mighty fortress.

The Brick	The Mortar
Pondering	Self-control
	Selflessness

Passion

When I heard these things, I sat down and wept.

—Nehemiah 1:4

Have you ever found yourself sitting at your kitchen table, head in hands, tears streaming, shoulders heaving, heart breaking with grief and concern over a child? Please tell me I am not the only one!

Nehemiah heard the distressing news about his people's safety, and he sank into a chair and wept. He had *passion*, and it was so great that the emotion overwhelmed and consumed him for days. In fact, his passion drove the rest of his story. It was the fuel that kept him focused on the task for which God had exclusively designed him.

I think moms are more like Nehemiah in their passion than in anything else. Nehemiah passionately loved his people. Moms passionately love their children. Passion made Nehemiah a bold and courageous leader for Israel. Passion will make you a bold and courageous mom for your children.

Nehemiah had a passion that drove him to action. You must be so passionate about your child that it moves you to tears and drives you to action. Passion may be the third brick in your wall, but it is a foundational one, and all the other bricks rest upon it. Passion is a strong and compelling emotion that will motivate you to dare to parent in today's world.

> ### Brick #3
> ### Passion
> A Passionate Mom must be passionate about her child.

Passion is powerful, and moms by nature are passionate about their children. I will never forget the first time I felt invaded by a passion from some place deep within that left the rational side of me questioning who I had become. My first child, Megan, was only four months old, so my hormones were still on the skittish side. We were taking our first trip to visit family, just she and I. I had gracefully navigated airport security *with* all the baby paraphernalia and *without* a peep from my well-behaved newborn. I was feeling so competent, and I settled rather smugly into my seat with little precious, thinking, *I can do this; what is the big deal?*

We taxied to the runway. The engines began to roar. My seat began to shake. Then the plane lurched forward and began to race down the runway with increasing speed. My heart lurched right with it and took off before the plane did. I was startled and confused. I felt as if the revving engine had somehow connected to my heart. The noise and speed escalated, and so did the sound and pace of my heart beating. My mind was not my own, and every nerve I had was screaming, *YOU CANNOT PROTECT YOUR BABY ON THIS PLANE—GET OFF NOW!*

Just when you think you have it together as a mom, you realize you don't.

Well, the alien that invaded has never left me. Thankfully, my hormones have calmed down a bit, but that passion to protect, fight for, nurture, and love my children is always there. For better or worse. And when my children are in trouble, my passion pours out in tears—just as it did for Nehemiah.

THE INTENSE AND INFINITE PASSION OF A MOM

As women, we can have some really unexplainable teary moments. My husband, Mark, loves to laugh when he tells the story of the first time I cried in our marriage. We were still in our first year, only nine months into our marriage, but I was already six months pregnant. Mark came home from work to find me in a puddle of tears, sobbing hysterically. To his credit, his first reaction was concern that something might have happened to the baby. My response to his concern was to sob irrationally and say without any explanation as to why, "I just wish it were Christmas!" It made perfect sense to me. Christmas was my favorite time of the year, and if it were only Christmas, I would be within weeks of finishing work and delivering the baby. Whatever concern he had during that first teary moment of our marriage evaporated into amusement.

As skeptical as a lot of men may be about the validity of women's emotions, I believe that God created us to be creatures of intense and infinite passion. It is that passion that drives us to instinctively desire to protect and provide for our children. Our passion is what makes each of us that intense mama bear we've all seen standing on her hind legs and pawing the air. Think about it. When and why do you cry for your children? Do you have a child with a lifelong medical condition? I do, and I have cried watching her physically fight just to feel well. Do you have a child who has been left out or socially hurt by others? I do, and I have cried with her in her humiliation and anger. Do you have a child who didn't make a team, didn't get a part in a play, or just worked really hard for something he or she didn't get? I did on all three counts, and my heart was more broken with disappointment than theirs. Do you have a child making unwise, rebellious choices with scary consequences? I did, and my gut ached with fear while my eyes dripped with tears.

But our passion also makes our love infinite. Recently, my sister-in-law Karen's mother became really ill and had to spend some time in an assisted-living facility for rehabilitation. Karen flew home to visit her mom and assess her care. As she spent the next few days at the facility in observation, she noticed two other patients in particular. They were physically able and were often out and about the facility, so my sister-in-law soon came to recognize them. They also had another distinguishing factor: they both carried baby dolls. Karen is very tenderhearted, and it really touched her to see these elderly women caring for their baby dolls.

She mentioned this to one of the nurses and asked why the two women carried dolls. The nurse told her that both of them had lost some mental capacity. Neither one could remember much of their lives or their children's lives. But instinctively, they still yearned for the children they didn't know and were greatly comforted when in possession of their baby dolls. Is that amazing? The memory of their children was gone, but the passion for them was still there. And it must have been an intense passion because they became distraught if they didn't have their "babies." The passion to protect and nurture was still intact. The mind forgets, but the heart always protects, always perseveres. Love never fails; it is infinite. These aged mothers couldn't remember what they loved, but they still loved passionately.

A mother's love is passionate—intense and infinite—from beginning to end!

Nehemiah's story is filled with the same passion. We see it in the very beginning of his book, where he wrote that he sat down and wept at the news of his people. We will see it all the way through to the end of his story. His passion never failed because it was fueled by love. Nehemiah loved his God and loved his people, and he would do anything for them—he would protect them by building the wall; he would trust God; and he would persevere to completion.

Love never fails, and Nehemiah was not going to fail because his passion was firmly rooted in his love. Mixing love into our mortar is an easy one because it is so natural for a mom, and love will help us keep that brick of passion in place.

Love: strong affection and tender concern for another

First Corinthians 13 says, "Love is patient, love is kind. . . . It always protects, always trusts, always hopes, always perseveres. Love never fails." Indeed, love *is* unfailing, and that quality can make if painful. When we love deeply, it is painful to watch our children make mistakes or suffer.

I recently discovered a rebellious streak in one of our children. It came as a painful surprise to my husband and me. It was also a strong source of discouragement to me as I was writing this book on parenting. I really struggled with this verse about love too.

Love always protects, but it is a struggle to protect a child when he or she makes unwise choices.

Love always trusts, but it is a struggle to trust that God has a plan for a disobedient child and that he is in total control of the details of the plan, no matter how scary it looks.

Love always hopes, but it is a struggle to hope that a child will have a future that looks very different from the present— a future relationship restored to the sweetness that it was in the past.

Love always perseveres, but it is a struggle every single day to persevere without being overcome by fear and sorrow.

Love never fails. Is that a promise? I want to believe, but I get scared that I will fail.

Love hurts, but love also hopes. As moms, we must love intensely and infinitely, persevering in hope that our love will not fail.

Confession

I am not a very good passionate mom. My trust is weak and easily gives way to fear, and I deeply fear that I will fail as a mom. As Nehemiah cried over his people, I passionately cry over my children. But that is where my likeness to Nehemiah ends. I haven't mastered the trust and hope. I have the passion and tears, but I am caving to the fear instead of persevering in the hope. And the worst of it is that my fear paralyzes me and I get confused about what actions to take in times of need.

It is so easy to talk about something—it is so hard to take action. But that is exactly what Nehemiah did.

PASSION TAKES ACTION

Nehemiah's people were in trouble, and it is clear he felt passionately about it. There is nothing amazing in that. When our children are in trouble, we can be just as passionate. What is amazing and an inspiration to me is what Nehemiah did with his passion. He did not allow himself to be permanently overwhelmed. He did not freeze in fear. Nehemiah took initiative. He poured his passion into action—marvelously organized, calculated, purposeful action. I want that kind of passion, the kind that forces me into fearless action and results in a lifelong plan for parenting with purpose so I will produce wise, healthy, relational, and purposeful adult children.

Initiative: the ability to recognize what needs to be done—and do it

If you know Nehemiah's story, you know his passion was about to erupt into a *whole lot* of action. It would fuel the initiative he would need to build Jerusalem's wall, to protect his people, to deflect attack, and to persevere to the end. A Mom needs the same. She needs initiative to funnel her passion into action. It is a character quality that can free a mom from panic and fear and set her in motion to protect and provide her child with a future.

PERCEPTION AND PONDERING SPARK PASSION

I was and am passionate about protecting, nurturing, and training my children. But in one particular case, I missed an opportunity to nurture and train because I was unperceptive. It was one of my bigger perception misses.

I have a child who was always so easy, so compliant, and so adored for good behavior that it never crossed my mind that he could be anything less than perfect. At the same time that this perfect one was morphing into a teenager, I became distracted by another child we had just adopted. The new addition to the family was justifiably in need of a lot of attention, and I gave it, passionately. The other children's needs paled in comparison, and I became unperceptive of those needs. I totally missed what was going on in my quiet child, and I never gave it a thought. I forgot to ponder because I was unperceptive. I couldn't be passionate about his needs because I was unaware that there *was* a need.

Years later . . . such guilt. Such passion and tears at the kitchen table, head in hands—you get the picture. I eventually perceived what I had failed to observe. We all make mistakes; I can attest to that.

A lack of perception can be a deterrent to passion. Conversely, proficient perception can drive passion.

Take Nehemiah, for example. He obviously was passionate about his people or he wouldn't have been so upset. But had he not been pondering them over the years, would he have even thought to ask his brother about them? If he had been distracted and not listening, would he have perceived the problem? But he did, and it drove the man's heart. It fueled a fire that expanded his capacity far beyond himself. Passion can do the same for us.

Take your passion and put it into action—after you have perceived and pondered what to take action about!

PASSION DRAINERS

I have never met a woman who gave birth devoid of passion and love for her child, although I am sure some exist. I have, however, met women who have lost a bit of that passion. I don't think they meant to lose it; it just happened along the way. Their passion was just imperceptibly drained out of them. I have sprung many a slow passion leak. I have had all kinds of great intentions of what kind of family we would be, the memories we would make, the lessons I would share, the manners I would instill, the daily dinners I would cook, the words of love and joy I would impart.

But sometimes, many times, things get in the way; stuff happens; life's trials can get us off track. Then that happy, iridescent bubble pops, and we become overwhelmed and discouraged. Many moms feel like failures; they only see the parts of life that got away from them—the things they didn't do instead of all the things they did do, their parenting triumphs. I have often felt like a failure. And that discouragement can plummet a mom's passion to near nonexistence.

Trials and tribulations cannot be avoided. Everyone will

experience suffering in one form or another: dealing with a difficult child or a husband addicted to pornography; caring for an aging parent, a seriously ill or handicapped child, or a needy friend or sibling; divorce, job loss, or financial difficulties; or cancer, an unexpected tragedy, or the loss of a life. Troubles can make you physically, mentally, and emotionally weary. And weariness is a huge threat to passion. I do not have solutions for the varied and complicated trials of life; however, there are a few things we can do to take care of ourselves and protect ourselves from passion leaks.

- *Practice self-awareness.* A mom must be aware of the potential drain and approach stressors with balance and perseverance.
- *Practice conservative time management.* If you know that your days will be unpredictable and potentially exhausting, pad your calendar. That means build in extra time for everything so that if you don't use it, you can rest or regroup.
- *Maintain realistic expectations.* You must allow yourself to let go of anything that is not necessary, because you may not be able to do all that you saw yourself doing as a mom. For example, it is okay to say no to making cupcakes for the class party or babysitting a friend's child.
- *Be flexible.* You may be called to sacrifice time and energy to serve someone else who needs you. And if you are called, you must accept it and be flexible to changing your expectations without bitterness or envy toward others who do not share your trials.

- *Embrace hope.* Romans 5:3–4 says that "suffering produces perseverance; perseverance, character; and character, hope." Know that every trial is a season of suffering. Find comfort in the knowledge that you are building perseverance, character, and hope.
- *Rejoice in serving.* Remember that you are a passionate mom who loves deeply. It is a privilege and a joy to share that passion with others by loving them, devoting yourself to them, and serving them. Romans 12:9–13 tell us, "Love must be sincere. Hate what is evil; cling to what is good. Be devoted to one another in love. Honor one another above yourselves. Never be lacking in zeal, but keep your spiritual fervor, serving the Lord. Be joyful in hope, patient in affliction, faithful in prayer. Share with the Lord's people who are in need. Practice hospitality."

THE PASSIONATE MOM MUST HAVE PASSION

Nehemiah had passion for his people. His passion drove him to action—he was not about to stand by and let his people suffer. He was going to take the initiative and find a way to provide security for them because he loved them. Nehemiah did not allow the enormity of the problem to overwhelm him or confuse him. We will see in the next chapter that he remained passionately hopeful by pouring his passion into prayer that God would provide a way for his people—and that God would use *him* to do it.

Is your passion a bit drained right now? Have you used

perception and pondering to fuel your passion? Is your passion being funneled into action to protect and provide for your child?

If you choose to zero in on your child's life—to really try to train your child "in the way he should go"—you will need passion (Prov. 22:6). It won't be easy because passionate love does not allow us to back away from difficult tasks; it pushes us to take on challenges that are out of our comfort zones. And when that happens—when you have to do something beyond what you know you can do—that is when you learn to *pray*, believing that God can do the amazing task of raising children through you. Prayer is the next brick in the wall.

The Brick	The Mortar
Passion	Love
	Initiative

Prayer

I've always wanted to adopt. I believe my desire began at age fifteen while I was working with underprivileged kids. There was a boy named Jason whom I had the hardest time sending home every night. I just wasn't ever sure what kind of condition he'd come back in.

My husband, however, was pretty content with three healthy children. I failed at several attempts to interest him and finally resorted to plan B, which should have been plan A.

I prayed that the Lord would just drop a child in my lap.

I knew my husband would never refuse divine intervention. I believed it was possible. So I told my sister, Kathie, to pray for God to drop a child in my lap.

A year later she called and asked me to go look out my living room window. When I asked why, she said, "Do you see the church from your window? That's your 'lap.' That church is having a camp for thirty children from Russia who are available for adoption."

An opportunity had presented itself.

The church was looking for host families for the kids. There was no obligation to adopt, but you would have the opportunity to adopt the child if the Lord so moved. Mark said I could *host* all I wanted. So we signed up and requested a boy. I thought we would even up the male-to-female ratio in the house. I was out of town when we received the picture of a five-year-old boy. My husband was really excited!

God was moving through my husband.

This is it, I thought. The boy's age was perfect because my youngest, Mark Jr., was seven at the time. Our family would be complete—Megan, age thirteen; Emily, age eleven; Mark, age eight; and a new son, age five!

And then we got the news that the judge in his district thought he was too young for such a trip.

A door closed.

My girls and I decided to volunteer for the camp anyway. We attended daily and played with the children who were allowed to come from Russia. It did not take Megan and Emily long to fall in love with two little girls, a little blonde four-year-old and her redheaded, six-year-old sister. My girls begged Mark to go meet the girls in case their host family didn't adopt them, so that we could. He laughed at the notion of having four girls in the family but finally relented. He couldn't help adoring them and agreed to adopt them if their host family did not.

God was moving through my husband.

The camp ended, and the children went back to Russia.

We waited and waited to hear if the host family had made a decision to adopt the girls. They had.

A door closed.

We were all so sad, but God was moving, and he had changed my husband's heart. He wanted to adopt not one but two children. So we signed up for the next camp to host two children! And we began to pray as a family that these two would be ours.

This time I was home when the pictures arrived, and I eagerly opened the e-mail to see a precious girl and boy. And then my heart sank. The girl and Emily were almost exactly the same age—just two weeks apart—and the boy and Mark Jr. were just nine months apart.

All I could think was no, no, this would never work! I would have two girls turning thirteen within the year, and all five would be teenagers at the same time! Not to mention all the advice we had been given about disrupting the birth order of our children.

I closed the door.

I called the agency immediately and told them that we would like to adopt children younger than ours. I assumed Mark would agree, but—wouldn't you know—he didn't. He came home that night, took one look at the pictures, and said, "Well, don't you think we should at least meet them?" What could I do? If my husband, who hadn't even been interested in adopting, was open to it, who was I to say no?

God moved through my husband. And we prayed for the discernment to know it this was God's will for our family.

We agreed to host Yulia and Yura. They arrived a few days after Christmas on a Sunday night and looked positively pitiful. They had nothing with them but what they wore—layers of mismatched, worn, winter clothes. We had bought them clothes, knowing they would come with nothing. And I knew they looked small for their ages, but everything I bought was huge. Yulia was twelve years old but needed a size 6x. On top of what appeared to be delayed growth due to malnutrition, Yura was sick with a chest full of congestion and a terrible cough. I became choked with guilt. What if this didn't work? The camp was only three weeks, and we had to make a decision by Friday so they could find other families to meet them if we said no to adopting. What if no one adopted them?

Fear—worry—anxiety—panic.

I woke up the next morning, Monday, in a panic. All was quiet, and that was miracle number one. Kathie; my brother-in-law, Greg; and my niece and nephew were staying with us for Christmas and to meet the children—putting the house total at eleven. I sat at my kitchen table, attempting to get a grip on the panic that threatened to overwhelm me, and opened my Bible randomly—I repeat, *randomly*—to Hebrews 11. There I read:

FAITH IN ACTION

- Now faith is confidence in what we hope for and assurance about what we do not see. This is what the ancients were commended for.
- By faith we understand that the universe was formed at God's command, so that what is seen was not made out of what was visible.

- By faith Abel brought God a better offering than Cain did.
- By faith Enoch was taken from this life, so that he did not experience death.
- By faith Noah, when warned about things not yet seen, in holy fear built an ark to save his family.
- By faith Abraham, when called to go to a place he would later receive as his inheritance, obeyed and went, even though he did not know where he was going. And by faith even Sarah, who was past child-bearing age, was enabled to bear children because she considered him faithful who had made the promise.
- By faith Abraham, when God tested him, offered Isaac as a sacrifice.
- By faith Isaac blessed Jacob and Esau in regard to their future.
- By faith Jacob, when he was dying, blessed each of Joseph's sons, and worshiped as he leaned on the top of his staff.
- By faith Joseph, when his end was near, spoke about the exodus of the Israelites from Egypt and gave instructions concerning the burial of his bones.
- By faith Moses' parents hid him for three months after he was born, because they saw he was no ordinary child, and they were not afraid of the king's edict.
- By faith Moses, when he had grown up, refused to be known as the son of Pharaoh's daughter.

- By faith the people passed through the Red Sea as on dry land; but when the Egyptians tried to do so, they were drowned.
- By faith the walls of Jericho fell, after the army had marched around them for seven days.
- By faith the prostitute Rahab, because she welcomed the spies, was not killed with those who were disobedient.

And what more shall I say? I do not have time to tell about Gideon, Barak, Samson, and Jephthah, about David and Samuel and the prophets.

These were all commended for their faith, yet none of them received what had been promised, since God had planned something better for us so that only together with us would they be made perfect.

By faith . . . "since God had planned something better for us so that only together with us would they be made perfect."

God moved.

I am not stupid; in other words, I knew this process would entail putting my faith into action. By faith I needed to walk through the next four days and see what God revealed. If we decided not to adopt, then *by faith* I would have to trust that God had another plan for these children. If we adopted, then *by faith* I would have to trust that our family could handle it.

I prayed. And panic gave way to peace.

So the next day, Tuesday, I took Yulia and Yura to see my friend Tatyana, who spoke Russian. I was dying for a little verbal communication and had a million questions I wanted to ask them. Tatyana chatted away, and the children were so excited to find someone who understood them. She asked about their parents and how they came to be in the orphanage, and then she got really excited. As she translated from Russian to English, she shared that there were three more siblings in their family, all younger.

Uh-oh, I thought. *God is closing the door.*

I knew without a doubt that we could not adopt five children. But I continued to ask questions through Tatyana, trying to get to the bottom of how Russia allowed only two children to come to the camp when they don't allow the separation of siblings. How old were they? Where were they? They were ages five, four, and one. Yura said that when he was in the hospital in Russia, two of his sisters came in from another orphanage to get a medical exam because they were going to Florida. That was the only time he had seen them in over a year. The one-year-old was in his orphanage.

My wheels were spinning. "Florida?! What do they look like?" I asked. Tatyana asked and told me one had blonde hair, one red. With dawning suspicion I asked, "What are their names?" They had the same names as the two girls we had fallen in love with in the prior camp! After much excitement and identification through pictures, it was confirmed that Yulia and Yura were the older siblings of those girls. They were already adopted by this time, and living one mile from our house. The agency had no idea that the children were related; the two sets of children had different last names and were in different orphanages two hours apart. But both sets of siblings were chosen to attend camps for the same city on the other side of the world!

God answered our prayer for discernment and made clear that this was his will for our family.

We adopted Yulia and Yura, who became Hannah and Grant. They no longer live hours from their sisters—they're just a mile away! And across the street from their two sisters, another family adopted the last child in Yulia and Yura's family, the baby. It still amazes me that all five children are in the same city. To this day I ponder at times what this new life will bring all of them individually and together, thousands of miles from where they were born, now in different families, but strangely, still together.

I really don't know what my life would look like without prayer. And I hope you can see from this story that prayer is not about getting what you want; it's about being open to what God wants. Prayer, as we will see from Nehemiah, is the starting place for putting faith into action.

NEHEMIAH PRAYED

"When I heard these things, I sat down and wept. For some days I mourned and fasted and prayed before the God of heaven."

—Nehemiah 1:4

He heard; he wept; for days he prayed. Such a short verse and yet so important because of how he began—in prayer, trusting God. Prayer is the response to passion. If you are passionate about your child, pray for him or her. Passion is the force that drives us to our knees—prayer is poured out from that passion and sent to the One, the only One, who is in control of the situation and your child.

Brick #4
Prayer
A Passionate Mom will pour her passion into prayer because she trusts that every detail of her child's life is in God's hands.

Nehemiah had so much passion for his people that he prayed *for days*. Now, that is passion! He prayed with passion and love for his people to the only One who could take care of them— God. He had other choices. He could have jumped right into planning. He could have called a meeting, set up committees, raised money, and *taken charge*. But he did not. Nehemiah was too wise. Whatever past experiences God had provided him, Nehemiah had learned his lessons from them well. He knew he needed the Lord to be the leader of his expedition, so he prayed.

PRAY OR PANIC? WHAT DO YOU DO?

The other choice Nehemiah could have made was to go to pieces. He could have surrendered to panic over the insoluble challenge of overcoming the devastation of his people's security. He didn't. He was too wise and self-controlled.

Not me. I would have had a meltdown under the pressure. I probably would have subjected my husband to days of "How am I going to do this?"

What about you?

—————— **Confession** ——————

My go-to answer is panic, not prayer. I can be pretty good with those bricks of perception, pondering, and passion. Like Nehemiah, I'll have a good cry, but then, as the tears subside, my mind takes off as if it's in a NASCAR race, around and around and around, but not in a good way. Every circle around the track is a different scenario of the situation, in a thousand shades of depressing gray. I overreact in fear.

I work with several moms at iMOM. We spend a lot of time talking about our children as we brainstorm about content to research and develop for iMOM's daily e-mail. Fear, worry, and panic over our children are recurring topics. So we posted this question on Facebook: When you worry about your child, what do you worry about?

Here are some of the answers we got:

- I am so afraid . . .
  - she won't get into the college she wants.
  - he won't make the team.
  - she will be left out.
  - he might be drinking.
  - she won't be able to keep up; it's too hard.
  - he just can't focus.
  - he is being influenced by the wrong kids.
  - she won't stand up for herself.
  - he is taking advantage of her.
  - she will be teased.

- [because] he seems so down.
- something is going on at school.
- I am not doing enough.
- [because her classmates] are so mean to her.
- [because the other kids] just don't understand him.
- this will affect his future.
- having Celiacs [*sic*] could affect her future socially.
- she will end up with depression.
- [of] how the men in their lives will treat them.
- that they will have a freak accident.
- for their safety: at school, in the front yard, riding their bikes, and when they are away from me in general. It's a scary world out there!
- for their ability to know the difference between right and wrong when an adult is not around.
- about whether my preemie will be "normal." But then again, what is normal, anyway?
- about bullying at school.
- about the world they will grow up in . . . all the shootings and people going missing. The world is not a safe place anymore.
- [of their] being teased, getting hurt, kidnapped, or sick.
- [about] when they will accept the Lord as their personal Savior.
- [of] *everything*! I am a constant worrier and get myself so worked up sometimes I almost could have a panic attack!

And on top of all these responses, other worried moms posted these concerns:

- Will she be safe when she's out with her friends?
- Will he be safe when he is driving?
- My daughter has histiocytosis. I worry this disease will hurt her.
- How will others treat him and how will that impact who he is and what he believes?
- Will they have a strong faith in God?
- I worry that I am not teaching them enough in the time that I have.
- I worry that someone will take my daughter, and I worry that my son will get mixed up with bad influences.
- I'm a single mom to four sons so I worry about *everything*!

The worrying never stops!

THE CIRCLE OF FEAR . . . WORRY . . . ANXIETY . . . PANIC

Most of my worries follow a little pattern that can spiral out of control without me even noticing. It springs up as a little pang of fear; it then picks up speed, swirling into worry around my brain; next it spins me downward in a funnel of anxiety, till I bottom out in a puddle of panic. When I land, I am a mess—depleted, confused, and useless.

The circle of fear . . . worry . . . anxiety . . . panic is a circle I want out of! Accomplishing this requires awareness of how and when and why I fall into the circle. So here is my best attempt at explaining how this happens. Your circle may develop differently. Feel free to adapt the circle to fit your understanding of yourself. The point is awareness. If you are aware of how your fear begins, you can head off panic and end up a *useful* rather than *useless* mom.

The circle can be applied to everything that produces fear in your life, not just parenting. A year ago our house flooded during a storm that just happened to pop up while we were getting a new roof. It has been a year. We are a bit weary from sorting, moving, assessing, insurance battles, more moving, and so forth. Well, guess what? It is rainy season again, and there was another storm. No flood this time, just a little leak in the roof—the new roof. When I saw it, I did not panic because I was with the builder and was assured he was taking care of it.

Several days later my husband was walking out to go to the house, and I told him to double-check and make sure they fixed the roof. Unfortunately, I left out any attempt to reassure him that it was just a little leak that the builder was well aware of. He flat-out went from fear to panic in one leap. The roof and rain are now triggers for panic due to the still-raw emotions from the expense and time of our year in limbo. Before I knew it, e-mails were flying as fast as killer bees. Fear usually has triggers. Triggers cause us to jump to a heightened state of concern based on fear from a prior experience.

The circle begins with fear.

Fear: a distressing emotion aroused by impending danger, evil, pain, whether the threat is real or imagined; the condition of being afraid

Way too many of my thoughts seem to fit this description. Perhaps it is because of the ages of my children: they're big. Little children, little problems; big children, big problems. Perhaps it is because I don't trust. Maybe it is because I like things to be under control, and we cannot always control life or our children. Whatever the case, distressing emotions are not healthy and can lead to the second stop on the circle, *worry*.

Worry: to give way to fear; to allow one's mind to dwell on troubles; to torment oneself with disturbing thoughts; to fret

Fear does not lead to worry unless you give it a license to. In other words, the circle could easily end at fear. When you worry, it is because you are giving way to fear. Worry is fraught with tormenting thoughts that do not need to exist. Worrying can become a very bad habit. It can easily grow until it consumes our thoughts and gives birth to the third stop around the circle, *anxiety*.

Anxiety: uneasiness of mind caused by fear of danger or misfortune that develops into a state of apprehension and psychic tension

I promise I did not make up these definitions. They are in the dictionary. Anxiety is a state of *apprehension* and *psychic tension*. This is where we become useless to our children and the situation. We are so wrapped up in the problem that no matter what happens we see and react to it as if it were catastrophic. You may be in this state if more than one of your children is telling you, "Mom, calm down. It's not that big a deal." By this point in the circle, you are spinning faster and are well on your way to the final phase, *panic*.

Well, the panic may be sudden, but trust me: it was

preceded by the slow and stealthy growth of fear, worry, and anxiety. Please note the description of a mom with "hysterical or irrational behavior." Have you ever witnessed a mother chew a coach out for not playing her child? She panicked because her child was not getting the opportunity for success that she wanted him to have. Have you ever had a teacher tell you how a mother screamed at her because her

Panic: a sudden overwhelming fear, with or without cause, that produces hysterical or irrational behavior

child failed a test? That mom panicked because she thought her child was not achieving. She was anxious about her child's success to the point of irrational behavior, and she was miserable in her state of apprehension and psychic tension. That mom, in that moment, was useless to her child.

Ladies, we do not want to be that mom.

I have a relationship with a friend that has transcended the norm. We both adopted teenagers around the same time. Teenagers can be challenging in general; adopting them can be even more challenging. A good mom support team can be lifesaving. My friend Lesley was just that for me. She was a year ahead of me in her adoption and was a great source of perspective when I was losing mine.

Adopted teenagers often, but not always, have been through years of difficulties. These years impact and affect their thinking and behavior and as a result can create some stressful situations. Pondering was especially necessary during these times, and I did a lot of it. My pondering often gave way to panic—and I confess I panicked a lot. When I did, Lesley would say to me, "Pull up, Susan, pull up." She had coined this phrase, and we used it regularly throughout our "therapy" together. She decided that to get a really good view of a situation, you had to "pull up" for an aerial view. When we panic, we descend so that we can't see the forest for the trees. We get lost in the details and spend our time frantically dodging the thorny branches as we fly through the forest. Instead, we should pull up, safely avoiding all those branches, to see the problem for what it really is.

If I were a psychologist, I am sure I could explain that panic comes from a different part of the brain, and therefore our thinking is radically altered, or something like that. I only know that when I operate out of panic, I am a lot less productive. When I grab ahold of myself and pull up, I do, in fact, see the situation differently and am able to ponder. Panic is the antithesis to pondering. One occurs with desperate and clouded vision from below, and the other occurs with patient and clear vision from above.

How do you pull up for an aerial view when your child has shot a missile through your heart and you are bleeding out of the fuselage so fast that you're seeing red and falling rapidly? Again, I am neither a psychologist nor a pilot, but my answer is to focus on something much higher and bigger than anything I have going on—God. He is bigger than my child and my problem. In looking up in prayer, I remember that there is nothing I am experiencing that hasn't been experienced a million times before. This is life. This is life with children. Once I look up, I usually find I have climbed to thirty thousand feet and am appropriately prepared to look down at my situation rationally.

Nehemiah never panicked. He pulled up by praying for days. And because he didn't waste any time on panic, he remained focused enough to see his plan and execute it. A passionate mom, when faced with panic, will pull up and regain the ability to ponder.

PRAYER IS GUARANTEED
PANIC PREVENTION

So how did Nehemiah avoid panicking? Nehemiah, as many moms would, had himself a good cry, but he did not allow his grief and concern to convert to fear. He capped off the panic and downloaded all his passion into fervent prayer. The Bible says he continued to mourn, but he also took action: he fasted and prayed for days. This is invariably where I would go wrong. Oh, I would take action too: I would fret about how I could rectify the situation. I would come up with solution options. I would call a multitude of friends and bounce my proposed solutions off of them. I would analyze their answers. And then I would take the action that I concluded was the answer to the problem. Are you catching all the "I" actions in these statements?

We are a DIY generation. We think Do-It-Yourself is the way it gets done. It is all about "I." Well, it's not. In fact, thinking we can do it is the very thing that produces anxiety, apprehension, and psychic tension because it creates a lot of pressure to perform. We have forgotten *humility*. Nehemiah knew that saving his people was a problem that was bigger than him. He knew he didn't have the answer, and he didn't waste time trying to figure it out. He went straight to the Lord *in humility*. Nehemiah knew something we have forgotten. He knew that if he humbled himself before God, God would lift him up in due time.

Humble yourself.

Do you mean that I have to accept that I do not have a solution? you may be thinking. *Give up my analyzing, searching, obsessing, planning? Do you mean I have to wait? Patiently? Praying and trusting God to do that which I think I can and must?*

You can and *you* must. That is pride. *Humble yourself.*

> **Humility:** recognizing that it is God who is responsible for what happens in life, not me

"I can and I must" are DIY pride. When I let go of my DIY pride, and humbly trust that God has the answer, then I can cast all my anxieties on him, because guess what? He cares for me—the Bible clearly says so!

"Humble yourselves, therefore, under God's mighty hand, that he may lift you up in due time. Cast all your anxiety on him because he cares for you" (1 Peter 5:6–7).

So the circle of fear . . . worry . . . anxiety . . . panic will come to an end with these four things:

- humility
- trust
- casting all my anxiety on God
- prayer

The only way to cast your anxiety on God is to pray. Prayer is the only guaranteed panic prevention. Nehemiah knew that, and I am learning that prayer requires two characteristics— humility and trust. And putting these two into the mortar will help with a lot more than just this one brick of prayer. Humility and trust will help keep all the bricks in our walls.

BUT I DON'T KNOW HOW

Some of you may be thinking there has to be another way. *Prayer is so inconclusive—I can think of several other ways to build this wall.* Let me just point out that if you are thinking this way, you are rationalizing and working up an excuse to take back control.

Trust: believing that God has the answers and will take care of me and my family

Some of you may be thinking, *Well, I really don't pray,* or *I really don't know how to pray.* Let me ask you: have you ever been in an emergency situation with your child? When your child's life is on the line, and you are rushing to the hospital with a six-inch gash oozing blood from his cracked-open head, do you not pray?! If you don't pray, then to whom are you talking as you plead for your child's life? Do any of these prayers sound at all familiar?

3:00 a.m.	*Please, Lord, please help this baby to sleep for just four hours.*
104 degrees	*Two degrees, Lord! Please bring the fever down even two degrees.*
2:00 a.m.	*Where are they? Lord, please, please bring them home safely.*
Number 15 is down on the field.	*Oh, Lord, help him get up! Please don't let him be hurt.*

30 points

*Oh, Lord, she has studied
so hard! She just needs a
few more points to get into
that school. Please help her
concentrate.*

I really cannot imagine raising children without God. If you don't think you pray but find that you can relate to some of these statements, then take a chance and try it. It does take a little practice, but the more you do it, the more you will love it. And Nehemiah has a great prayer format that will help you.

LEARN TO PRAY THE NEHEMIAH WAY

Prayer was Nehemiah's first step toward developing a plan of action to rebuild Jerusalem and its gates, so its people could live in safety.

Then I said:

"Lord, the God of heaven, the great and awesome God, who keeps his covenant of love with those who love him and keep his commandments, let your ear be attentive and your eyes open to hear the prayer your servant is praying before you day and night for your servants, the people of Israel. I confess the sins we Israelites, including myself and my father's family, have committed against you. We have acted very wickedly toward you. We have not obeyed the commands, decrees and laws you gave your servant Moses.

"Remember the instruction you gave your servant Moses, saying, 'If you are unfaithful, I will scatter you among

68

the nations, but if you return to me and obey my commands, then even if your exiled people are at the farthest horizon, I will gather them from there and bring them to the place I have chosen as a dwelling for my Name.'

"They are your servants and your people, whom you redeemed by your great strength and your mighty hand. Lord, let your ear be attentive to the prayer of this your servant and to the prayer of your servants who delight in revering your name. Give your servant success today by granting him favor in the presence of this man."

I was cupbearer to the king. (Neh. 1:5–11)

Prayer was Nehemiah's first step toward developing a plan for his people. You really cannot skip this step. Nehemiah's plan for building the wall was nonexistent until after he prayed. He knew better than to waste one minute trying to plan without consulting God. You will save a lot of time and energy if you do as he did. I have learned this lesson well—a plan with the Lord is a lot more productive than one without him. So before you start a plan—pray.

Another humble man of great power and influence felt the same way as Nehemiah about prayer. Abraham Lincoln said of prayer: "I have been driven many times to my knees by the overwhelming conviction that I had nowhere else to go. My own wisdom and that of those about me seemed insufficient for the day."*

That sums up about every day for me—my own wisdom does not seem sufficient for the day!

* Thinkexist.com, http://thinkexist.com/quotation/i_have_been_driven_many_times_to_my_knees_by_the/12574.html.

If we follow the example of these two great, humble leaders, perhaps we can turn our panic into purposeful parenting with a plan. Nehemiah began with humility by *adoring God*, proceeded with *confession*, recalled *with thanksgiving* the promise God had made to his people, and finished with a *supplication*, or request. For us it might look like this:

1. Adoration

Praising God with adoration is quite simple but very important to changing our attitude about who he is—before we launch into what we want from him. It reminds us of how great God is, and that can suddenly calm the fear threatening to engulf us. It humbles us as we realize how far superior his ways are to ours. *He knows what he is doing!* To praise God with adoration, simply fill in the blank in the statement:

Lord, you are _____.

Nehemiah filled it in with "God of heaven" and "the great and awesome God." I might fill it in with *Creator, enduring, loving, full of glory, mighty, merciful, faithful, the Protector.*

2. Confession

Confession adds to our position of humility. It reminds us that we are not perfect, and it helps us turn from our pattern of mistakes by confessing them to God. Confession reminds me that I don't have to carry my guilt. I can give it to God. He sees me, he knows I am a mess, and he forgives me. He wants me to acknowledge the mistakes, change, and move past them. This is crucial for me because without confession I don't move past my mistakes. I get caught reliving them. The guilt clouds my vision with negative, self-deprecating thoughts. This trap is so unnecessary and so easy to be free of. To confess you can begin with:

> *Lord, I confess that I* _____. *Forgive me and help me to* _____.

Nehemiah's confession was broad and profound in keeping with the despair he was feeling for his people at that moment in history. He said, "I confess the sins we Israelites, including myself and my father's family, have committed against you. We have acted very wickedly toward you. We have not obeyed the commands, decrees, and laws you gave your servant Moses" (1:6–7).

I most often fill in that first blank with confessions of angry words spoken to my children, neglecting my husband, wrong priorities, selfishness, impatience, envious thoughts, unkindness . . . You get the picture?

3. Thanksgiving

In his prayer Nehemiah expressed his thanks to God by recalling the promise that God made to his people. Nehemiah was so thankful that he didn't need to worry about his people because, he said, "they are your servants and your people, whom you redeemed by your great strength and your mighty hand" (v. 10).

Without thanksgiving in prayer I can miss the blessings God has brought me. We have to look for them. It sounds Pollyanish, but it is true. The more you practice giving thanks, the more blessed you become. Start with this:

Lord, thank you for _____.

I am thankful for so much: the technology of my pace-maker and the skill of my cardiologist, my children's good health, my husband's faithfulness, the house God has provided us, the opportunity to share through this book, the fellowship of my friends, the beauty of the view outside my window, the sound of the rain as I write this chapter.

4. Supplication (a fancy name for a request)

By the time I get to supplication—after adoration, confession, and thanksgiving—I am, usually, a totally different woman from the one who started to pray just a few minutes before. It is an amazing transformation, and it can take you right out of that circle of you-know-what and up to a beautiful view at thirty thousand feet. It can also totally change your mind about what you were going to request.

To *supplicate* means "to pray humbly; make humble and earnest entreaty or petition." So interesting that we are right back to that "humble" thing. Nehemiah said it like this: "Lord, let your ear be attentive to the prayer of this your servant and to the prayer of your servants who delight in revering your name. Give your servant success today by granting him favor in the presence of this man." Then he stated humbly. "I was cupbearer to the king" (vv. 11–12). All he really asked for was favor with "this man," the king. That's it. That was the extent of what he wanted from God. He knew that God could work it out, so he didn't ask for anything other than favor with the king.

It really is that easy. Simply ask:

Lord, I pray that _____.

My supplication tends to get a bit more detailed as I ponder my children one by one. And that is okay. God cares about our every concern and detail. See Resources (p. 231) for a link to the page on my blog susanme.com where you will find two printables to help you pray for your child: "10 Ways to Pray for Your Child" and "10 Ways to Pray for Your Teenager." Whatever you use or however you choose to pray, just do it.

DO NOT BE AFRAID TO PRAY

Another one of my favorite Bible characters lived in the same time period as Nehemiah and had success in a similar situation. She was a captive Israelite of such beauty that she was taken into the king of Persia's harem and ultimately made queen. Her name was Esther. She was not quite as confident as Nehemiah, perhaps because she was so very young. Her people, the Jews, were in great danger (a repeated theme). She alone had access to the king, and she alone could save them, but she was afraid. Her uncle chastised her for her fear, saying, "Do not think that because you are in the king's house you alone of all the Jews will escape. For if you remain silent at this time, relief and deliverance for the Jews will arise from another place, but you and your father's family will perish. And who knows but that you have come to your royal position for such a time as this?" (Es. 4:13–14).

My dear moms, do you know that you have come to a royal

position in your house for such a time as this? You and you alone have that mom passion to pray fervently about your children's future. Esther got the message. Despite her youth, she got out of the circle and gave up fear, worry, anxiety, and panic by turning to God in prayer. She, like Nehemiah and Abraham Lincoln, realized that her situation was much bigger than she was, but she also realized that she served a very big God.

Her answer to her uncle was a humble one: "Go, gather together all the Jews who are in Susa, and fast for me. Do not eat or drink for three days, night or day. I and my attendants will fast as you do. When this is done, I will go to the king, even though it is against the law. And if I perish, I perish" (vv. 15–16).

Do not let anything come between you and prayer. It may be awkward; it may be inconvenient; it may feel like a waste of time. Pursue it anyway. Find the way for you to pour out your heart to God. Intercede for your children. I find the best way to pray is to insert my child's name into verses from the Bible. Every request you ever need to make on behalf of your child can be found in his book. In the later chapter, "Interlude: Opening the Gates," I will give an example of this type of prayer for every gate discussed. Pray those prayers for your children over and over. You will never regret it.

CHILD BEARER TO THE KING

The last little thing that Nehemiah reported as he closed out the first chapter of his story was a very humble, "I was cupbearer to the king." Moms, you are child bearers to *the* King of kings. You have a noble and humble and precious and priceless job, just like Nehemiah. You are bearing and caring for God's dearest possessions—children. He will listen to your prayers, he will fuel your passion, and he will provide you with a plan to protect and provide your child with a future. Cast all your anxiety on him, because he cares for you and your children.

THE PASSIONATE MOM MUST PRAY

Nehemiah set the plan to rebuild the wall in motion by starting with prayer. This is interesting for such an important, powerful man. He had resources as the cupbearer to the king and easily could have become carried away with his own ability to make things happen. He did not. Nehemiah understood that no one but God could accomplish the building of those walls for the protection of his people. And we must understand that no one but God can help us to become the moms we need to be for our children.

Nehemiah perceived, so he pondered. He was passionate, so he prayed. He built that wall, and so can you.

The wall, the wall, the wall. There is so much fuss about the wall—but for good reason. There is more to the wall than bricks and mortar, much more to Nehemiah's passion than physical protection. We must pause to really perceive and ponder about this wall of his. Why exactly did Nehemiah build the wall, and what parallel does that have for us?

The Brick	The Mortar
Prayer	Humility
	Trust

Interlude

Building the Wall

The *wall* of Jerusalem is broken down . . . (1:3)

I went out . . . examining the *walls* . . . (2:13)

I went up . . . by night, examining the *wall* . . . (2:15)

Let us rebuild the *wall* of Jerusalem . . . (2:17)

We were rebuilding the *wall* . . . (4:1)

Will they restore their *wall*? (4:2)

So we rebuilt the *wall* . . . (4:6)

There is so much rubble that we cannot rebuild the *wall* . . . (4:10)

I stationed some of the people behind the lowest points of the *wall* at the exposed places . . . (4:13)

We all returned to the *wall*, each to our own work . . . (4:15)

The officers posted themselves behind all the people of Judah who were building the *wall* . . . (4:16–17)

I devoted myself to the work on this *wall* . . . (5:16)

I had rebuilt the *wall* and not a gap was left in it . . . (6:1)

So the *wall* was completed . . . (6:15)

—Nehemiah

THE WALL . . . THE WALL . . . THE WALL

In January 2010, for some reason—don't know why—I decided to study Nehemiah in the context of parenting. I know that sounds crazy, but I have always loved his story—and as the director of iMOM, I look for the mom angle in *everything* I do!

So with my "mom" glasses on, I began to ponder this story. Right away I could totally relate to Nehemiah. He had a sold-out passion for his people the way a mom is passionate about her children. His people were in a great danger, exposed to the world without protection, just like many of the children I see today.

And then it dawned on me that Nehemiah's concern for the wall was not related to physical safety alone. Nehemiah saw something else in the terrible devastation of the wall that I had missed. Something that paralleled the way I parent, in a way I had never thought about before.

WHY WAS NEHEMIAH SO UPSET ABOUT THE WALL?

What struck me about Nehemiah is how profoundly distraught he was about the news that the wall was broken down and the gates burned. His distress consumed him for days, to the point that he could do nothing but weep and pray. Certainly some of his concern was for the people's safety. In those days most cities built walls to protect inhabitants from the lawlessness of the land. Without the wall Nehemiah's people were vulnerable to enemy attack. Safety was a very good reason for concern. But I believe there was more to his grief than the people's *physical* safety.

There is also more to the story behind Nehemiah's passion for the wall.

Years before Nehemiah's time, the Israelites' king, Solomon, built a beautiful temple as the dwelling place for God. The Lord promised the Israelites that if they would follow his decrees, he would live among them, in the temple (1 Kings 6:11–13; 8:10–13). This promise meant much to the Israelites—it meant communion with God. However, like most of us, they struggled with obedience, and the consequence was clear: Nebuchadnezzar, king of Babylon, invaded Israel in 587 BC and destroyed the temple (2 Kings 25). He also carried multitudes of Israelites away from their homeplace as captives.

The Israelites were a people united by their faith in God. The point of their communion, the source of their faith, the place wherein they rallied together as a nation was the dwelling place of God—the temple. But that place of dwelling was gone because the temple was gone, the people were scattered, and their future hope was dwindling.

One by one, new kings came into play, and the Israelites were eventually allowed to return to Jerusalem. Once there, they made several attempts to rebuild their city. Finally, in 516 BC, the rebuilding of the temple was complete, but the remnant of people in Jerusalem was small and weak. Things were not going well when Nehemiah caught the news in 446 BC that the wall and gates were still in rubble and the people were in danger.

Without the wall, the rebuilt temple was at risk. Without the temple, the people's relationship with God was at risk. Without God, the people's eternal salvation was at risk. Their hope, their eternal future, and the heart of who they were were wrapped up in their ability to commune with God in the temple. I believe Nehemiah was deeply grieving not only for the physical safety of his people but for the *heart* of his people. He was grieving not just for their physical life but also for their eternal life. Nehemiah was upset because the wall needed to protect the heart of his people—the temple, the dwelling place of God—lay in ruins.

What about today? This is what I really pondered as I studied Nehemiah. You see, God no longer dwells in the temple of the Israelites. We are asked, by Paul, "Don't you know that you yourselves are God's temple and that God's Spirit lives in you?" (1 Cor. 3:16).

God dwells in the hearts of his people.

In the hearts of his people. In the heart of your child.

In Nehemiah's day, God resided in the temple; therefore, the protection of that temple, as a place of worship and relationship with God, was paramount. Today, God resides in the temple of the body. Hence, every person, every child, is a potential dwelling place for God. That means you, and that means your children. If God lives in the heart, there is communion with God; if there is communion, there is hope for a future eternally.

The temples that need to be protected today are the hearts of your children. The foundation for all those little temples is being laid in the home—*your home.* And if the foundation is to grow strong, it must be protected from attack. There must be walls and gates to keep it safe.

We should be concerned about the physical life of our children, but we should also be deeply passionate about their eternal life. How can you, as the wall that protects the heart of your child, be the best that you can as a mom?

You must be a strong wall and a wise gatekeeper.

DO CHILDREN EVEN NEED PROTECTION TODAY?

Today, we are so civilized that we don't need walls for protection . . . or do we? Our children are not being carried into slavery . . . or are they? Our homes are not being broken into and torn apart by enemies . . . or are they?

The enemy can come into your home craftily disguised. Pornography can steal a husband and father. Alcohol, marijuana, and other drugs can enslave a son. A daughter can be enticed to give her body away in exchange for popularity and adoration. The attack can be silent, but the results are the same—devastating destruction. I am talking physical, emotional, and life-altering destruction. It comes in many forms, so subtly that it goes unperceived until there is no time to ponder because the havoc is upon you. You cry out with passion and tears of regret because you couldn't see the forest for the trees. You couldn't see the big-picture goal of your parenting because you were caught up in the minutiae of life. Now, looking back, you clearly see that the path you were on was not the path you meant to be on. *Is this every mother's fear? Or is it just mine?* I often wonder.

YOU ARE NEHEMIAH TO YOUR CHILD

It is so interesting to me how naturally we become the walls to our children from the moment they come into the world. Your child was created in the safety of your womb. After birth, the safety of your arms is what keeps your child alive. God designed your child to be completely dependent on you. As an infant, he moves only when you move him. As a toddler, he goes out only when you open a gate and go with him. As a tyke, he leaves you only when he has your permission and complete knowledge of his destination. You are the walls of protection around your child, and you are the gatekeeper between your child and the world. You are Nehemiah to your child.

Now, I stopped at "tykes" here because it gets a lot more complicated as they grow up. Protecting older kids is more complex because there are so many more gates to the world for those tweens and teens to go through. At what age is it appropriate to have a sleepover or go to the movies alone? When do you let them have a cell phone? How about a boy-friend? With five teenagers, I could go on and on. These are the gates in the wall. Nehemiah was upset about the broken gates too. So we will get to those gates after we lay a few more bricks in the wall. We are passionate moms with a plan, and included in that plan is when and how to safely open the gates to our culture!

You Lay the Foundation

Please don't jump to the conclusion that this book is all about protecting your child from the big, bad world. Secluding your son or daughter from every imaginable potential or per-ceived danger is not the answer and *not* what this book is about. Eventually, your children must grow up and leave the nest. Having a wise plan to ensure that they are ready is the point of this book. That is what we need to be the best moms we can be.

Also, please don't think that Nehemiah's part was the whole deal. It was not; it was only half. You see, there was a man named Ezra who came before Nehemiah. Ezra laid the foundation, rebuilt the temple, and led the people back to God.

The foundation for your children will be their faith—and you will lay that foundation. You must be both Ezra *and* Nehemiah for them.

You can build the strongest walls possible to protect your children. But if you don't lay a solid foundation for what they believe, you will have missed your whole mission. Laying the foundation of faith should be every mom's number one goal. Your children will leave you one day to start lives of their own. You do not want them to leave empty-handed. They will need a moral compass, a passion for something beyond themselves, and a faith that can stand the test of time.

──────────── **Confession** ────────────

I confess that it was far easier for me to assess and address my children's physical, mental, and emotional progress than their spiritual progress. Every mom was concerned about her children's health and stature, their grades and their social prospects. There seemed to be clear measurements for these, such as how many inches they grew that year, the number of A's on their report cards, and the number of birthday party invitations on the refrigerator. I had to make a much more concerted effort to ensure spiritual development. It wasn't required by the state, like immunizations and school attendance were. And it wasn't required by my children, like playdates and birthday parties were. Our children's spiritual growth was a responsibility that fell solely on my husband and me, and when we got distracted, it didn't happen.

You must teach your child about God and about what you believe to be true, and the best place for you to learn how to do that is in church. Do not think you can do it alone. God created the family, and he ordained the church. Together they prepare children's hearts to fulfill God's plan for eternity.

YOU ARE THE PASSIONATE MOM

You are Nehemiah to your child. You are the wise mom who will lay the foundation of your child's faith. You are the Passionate Mom who will build the walls to protect your son or daughter. You are the passionate mom whose job it is to nurture and protect the little temple that was miraculously delivered into your life. Only you can perceive what life is throwing at your child and passionately protect and guide him or her through it. Only you can decide when to open one of the gates in the wall and expose your child to what lies on the other side. Only you will perceive, ponder, and pray as your child experiences different aspects of the culture through the gates you have opened. And only you will guide your child in wisdom as he learns to navigate the culture on his own.

I hope you are now even *more* passionate about building your wall. We have four bricks already laid—perception, pondering, passion, and prayer. And between those bricks, firmly cementing them in place, is the mortar of character qualities we need to possess in order to be Passionate Moms—alertness, availability, attentiveness, self-control, selflessness, love, initiative, humility, and trust. What will Nehemiah teach us next? A *very* difficult lesson for me—patience!

Patience

Patience is like my car keys—often lost, and found in the strangest places.

—Me

Everything takes patience; don't you think? Perception takes patience because sometimes children can chatter on for hours before they say something you really need to hear. Pondering takes patience because you have to be still and wait for the kaleidoscope of information to focus into meaning. Passion takes patience because you have to hold on to it until the right time to act. And brick #4, prayer, takes lots of patience. It takes patience to set aside time for an invisible God when very visible and precious little demands are tugging at our sleeves.

Confession

So, I am obligated to begin this chapter with a big, fat confession . . . I am not patient.

Patience is on my list of top three things I fail at on a consistent basis. I will share only a few of the dozens of my really good excuses for being impatient.

1. *Not Enough Time.* I don't have time! Husband, kids, work, volunteering—all take time; therefore, I don't have time to be patient for anything or anyone.
2. *Too Much to Do.* See #1. I cannot be patient because I am busy being productive.
3. *I Don't Like It.* I like being productive and being patient feels unproductive. So you see, patience is unnatural for me.

What are your excuses? If you have any creative excuses, I would like to borrow them to shore up my defense about why it is okay for me to be impatient. Sadly, I cannot blame, nor can I make excuses. Patience is a virtue that I have chosen not to value. And there is no way to justify my unwillingness to develop patience in my character. Patience is a brick that can make a mom great. If there were such a thing as a mom report card, I do believe patience would be worth at least two test grades.

Brick #5
Patience
A Passionate Mom has the ability to suppress restlessness or annoyance when confronted with delay.

PATIENCE REQUIRES TOLERANCE AND DISCIPLINE

"Genius is eternal patience."

—Michelangelo

Nehemiah did not share my neglect of patience. He is my hero in this area, and I will continue to strive to be like him. I am really hoping it is very clear to you that I do not hold myself up as a model Passionate Mom. I am a wannabe in the worst way. Nehemiah's story is so much better than mine, especially in the area of patiently waiting on God for the right opportunity. Nehemiah mourned, fasted, and prayed for some days, and then he immediately got his answer. Isn't that the way it goes?

Almost never. Nehemiah had to patiently wait, and wait, for days. It is clearly recorded that Nehemiah heard the news about his people in the month of Kislev in the twentieth year. This is spelled out in the beginning of chapter 1 of Nehemiah: "In the month of Kislev in the twentieth year, while I was in the citadel of Susa . . ." (v. 1).

In the beginning of chapter 2 of Nehemiah's story we learn that it wasn't until the month of Nisan that he finally got his chance to do something about his people's devastating situation. From Kislev to Nisan is four months. "In the month of Nisan in the twentieth year of King Artaxerxes, when wine was brought for him, I took the wine and gave it to the king" (v. 1).

It took four long months for Nehemiah's opportunity to present itself. Yet nowhere does it say that Nehemiah was stressed-out about it or that he lost hope. Nehemiah had caught a vision for a rebuilt wall and, like Michelangelo with the Sistine Chapel (four years!), he didn't care how long it took; he just knew it would happen. He handed the whole problem over to God in prayer and went on with his business in complete confidence that if God wanted to use him, he would present the opportunity.

This is only the beginning of Nehemiah's model of patience for us. You will see what trials the man came up against shortly. But he never lost it—he tolerated all kinds of attacks, internal squabbles, and delays. He had chosen to put on the virtue of patience for the long haul. He did this with great discipline, resisting the temptation to react to the people and circumstances around him. Instead, he patiently perceived, pondered, and then fixed his eyes on a plan.

It takes a great man (or mom) of character to quietly and steadily persevere through provocation, misfortune, delay, and even pain with fortitude and calm and without complaint or anger. I saw my daughter Emily do this once in an amazing way that was deeply convicting to me. She was the lead singer in a group of high school girls who were performing a particular number in an upcoming musical. In this production, singers were responsible for practicing and perfecting their own numbers outside of school. Well, getting this group together was like herding cats. Emily did not organize the number; she was asked to be in it by the girls because they needed a lead singer. She was already responsible for two other numbers. However, when this number did not look as though it was going to come together, the teacher came down on the group, and Emily in particular, because she was the lead singer, an officer in chorus, and his class aide.

The teacher challenged her to either get the number together or it was going to be pulled. So she stepped in and arranged for some extra rehearsals. A few of the girls did not like that; I am sure they felt Emily was taking over. Let me tell you how I felt! I was irritated. This child has Addison's disease, which means she has no adrenal function, so handling stress takes enormous effort and often an increase in steroids.

Emily patiently worked with whichever girls showed up for four weeks. Meanwhile, I was worried for her, emotionally and physically. This was a big show, rehearsals required an exhausting week of late nights, and school still started every morning at seven thirty.

The day for dress rehearsal finally came, and I was thankful to be working on the show so I could keep an eye out for her. My perception was on red alert—I just felt as if something was going on.

She had a flurry of costume changes, jumping from number to number, but when it was finally over and I had wrapped up what I was helping with, I went to help her. She was a little disconcerted. And her iPod and phone were missing.

Mama bear roared within me as visions of foul play flashed like an explosion in my brain. Emily saw it in my face and said, "Mom, please come help me get this stuff to my car." My heart melted at the weariness in her face, and my anger melted away as my concern for her refocused my attention. We gathered her stuff, and I walked her to her car.

"Mom," she said, "I need your help with something else, but I don't want you to be upset." Then she unzipped her garment bag and pulled out the dress from the "problem number." Somebody had stuck a huge wad of gum on the front of it. I looked at her face, so tired, so calm. "It will be okay, Mom. Can you get it out?" I reassured her that I could and would before the show the next day. (I actually didn't—*The Passionate Cleaner* is a book I will never write but need to read!)

The second she took off in her car, I got in mine and cried really angry, vengeful tears. But I knew that God was moving in my patient, sweet daughter, and that I should not intervene in this story. I did not act on my anger that night, but you'd better believe mama bear was on the prowl during the show the next night.

I had a job helping that evening, but I made sure to be at the side stage, where the singers got their mics, between songs to make sure she was okay. When I got there before the "problem number," I was informed that she was already wired up and backstage with the other girls. So I peeked my head in the door to check her out and give her a little squeeze.

Tolerance: the ability to remain unaffected by people or circumstances despite provocation or even pain

I will never forget what I saw. There, in the darkened wing, stood a dozen girls, holding hands while my daughter led them *in prayer.*

I shut the door and ran around to the back of the auditorium. Then I watched with tears and great pride a united group of girls having fun doing a very girlie number. The ominous feeling of impending doom was gone. And the knowledge that God was using Emily in a public school to pray with girls who may have never prayed before in their lives overwhelmed and humbled me. I have no doubt that had I lost my patience and interfered, the outcome of this story would have been quite different.

Sadly, I cannot claim the credit for having patience; that goes to my daughter. I kept mine in check not of my own volition, but in deference to hers.

Emily taught me that patience tempered with tolerance in the midst of pain and suffering can bring great blessing. And so this little bit of mortar comes from her. The character quality of tolerance will help you hold the brick of patience firmly in your wall. Tolerance will keep you from becoming annoyed with people or situations.

Without even looking it up, I could guess that the antonym for *tolerance* is *annoyance*. If you can tolerate people, you may not become so easily annoyed. Well, for a passionate mom like me, it takes great discipline not to jump onto the runaway emotion of being annoyed. Discipline also has to be in the mix. It is important to everything we do in life—praying, being patient, preparing, planning, persevering, and on and on.

Discipline: the ability to exhibit calm, controlled behavior

Whether it takes four weeks, four months, or four years, the passionate mom will tolerate all people and situations with great discipline so that she can be patient in all things.

THREE REASONS WHY YOU SHOULD BE A PATIENT MOM

1. Patience will make you wiser.

"Patience is the companion of wisdom."

—Augustine

Impatience has led me to make unwise parenting decisions. For example, I have often chosen to rescue my kids rather than patiently watch them fail. My children, in return, learned how to use this to their advantage. The scene would play out like this: One of my kids would have a paper or project, and sit there stumped. Soon it would get late, and I would get impatient and frustrated with the time. Finally, I'd jump in to help. Maybe even more than help. *Definitely* more than help. My impatience interfered with a lesson my son or daughter needed to learn. I should have let my child fail. Then he or she would have learned to work at it a little harder. Wisdom dictates that I discipline myself and patiently let my child work it out rather than jump to the rescue.

2. Patience will calm conflict.

"A hot-tempered person stirs up conflict, but the one who is patient calms a quarrel."

—Proverbs 15:18

I can be hot-tempered, and it has stirred up conflict in my home. Actually, my temper is more quirky than hot. I can let a lot roll off my shoulders, and then I hit a wall. When that happens, my patience evaporates and my temper goes from a comfortable 72 degrees to 110 in seconds flat. At other times my patience is like my car keys—I lose it often, and then I find it in the strangest places. I can lose my patience over a dozen silly things and then be super patient with something else. The regrettable reality is that many times I have created stress in my home over things that could have been settled more efficiently with patient words and a calm, objective demeanor. It causes me great pain to think about that.

3. Patience will circumvent sorrow.

"If you are patient in a moment of anger, you will escape a hundred days of sorrow."

—Chinese proverb

Even as I write this, I am amazed and ashamed that I am not better at being patient. Just today, one of my children successfully pushed a button that sent my husband and me into an impatient exchange of words. Looking back, I think the child knew exactly what he was doing, *and we didn't*. Children learn how to work their parents. This is especially true of younger siblings who get the benefit of watching their older brothers and sisters succeed and fail in their efforts to sway their parents.

My child read me today, made some innate calculations, and gambled that this would be a good time to get his way. He knew I was wearing thin on the subject at hand, and that if I lost my patience, he might succeed. Well, he did succeed with me; however, his father overheard the exchange and interceded by overriding me and vetoing my son's proposal. My son, knowing he was halfway there, did not give up. The result was a three-way discussion that, as I said, ended in an impatient exchange between my husband and me—*in front of my child*.

Children learn from watching us—for good or for bad. We must model the virtues we want to instill. If we don't, the exact opposite will occur. If they watch us enough times, we will be watching them lose their patience for hundreds of days to come, and that will bring much sorrow.

————

I haven't been totally without patience. However, I wish the lessons I learned about patience had stuck more. If I had become sold out to the necessity for patience and made practicing it a habit, I would have become more like some amazing mothers I know. Do you know that kind of mother—the unflappable kind who never gives in to impulse and is always calm?

This is one of those situations where I found patience in a strange place, and it paid off in a big way. As I mentioned before, we have two children we adopted when they were already almost teens. They had had difficult lives and had developed some coping mechanisms that were very trying, one of which was lying to cover up wrongdoings. At the time, I had five teenagers in the house. This left a lot of wiggle room for crazy lying, as there were so many options for who to blame.

During one particular period of misdeeds, I was frustrated and impatient to put an end to the three-ring circus. I was convinced one child was the perpetrator, but I could find no proof. So I worked it as hard as I could to solve the mystery. I perceived and I pondered ad infinitum. However, I was distracted and consumed by my desire to find the truth, so I don't recall how much I prayed and I certainly wasn't patiently trusting God for an answer. There seemed to be nothing I could do, and it disturbed me. Finally, I got to the point where I was just weary from it all. I gave up trying to figure it all out. I was done. I lay down on the couch, bracing myself for the hour when I had to pick the kids up from school and face my little lying-prone child again. Lying there, I just stared at the ceiling for a long time, Bible open on my chest, because I was too emotionally exhausted to even read it.

Then, in the stillness to which I finally submitted, it came to me. God knew the truth—every bit of it. All I needed to do was patiently wait for it to come out. The child was never going to confess unless moved to do so, and I could not make that happen. I was only frustrating myself.

Within minutes of this revelation, a plan came to me. I did know one thing for sure that the child had done—a minor thing. I could use that as my anchor for truth and then just *wait*. I just needed to be still!

When we got home from school, I said, "I know you have done something wrong. I am disappointed that you have lied about it. I do not want to argue or discuss it. I want you to go to your room, and when you are ready to confess it, I want you to write it on a piece of paper and bring it to me."

The child balked and quibbled. "What do you mean? What kind of thing? When did I do it?"

I refused to answer. And inwardly I enjoyed a little chuckle watching her squirm, trying to figure out which lie was the key to freedom from her room.

Patience was making me *wiser*.

Then I prayed. I prayed that the minor disobedience I knew about would be the final confession on that piece of paper, and that everything else the child needed to confess would come out before the minor one, including the big one that was so disturbing.

She produced a short list by the end of the day. The one known little lie was not on it. So I sent her back to her room.

The next day was Saturday and my child spent a long day in her room and produced several lists. That little anchor lie was still not on it, so I continued to tell her to go back upstairs because the lies on the list were not the lie I knew about. I was so elated, so freed up. This was great! I was calmly, patiently, effortlessly learning about all kinds of lies. The confusion that was pervading our household was being revealed in lists of confessions.

Patience was making me *calm in conflict.*

The child was now the frustrated one. I was not. For several days she refused to produce a list, accusing me of being crazy. I waited. Her anchor lie had not come out, so I knew for a fact there was at least one more in there. I patiently waited for what I knew to be true and let God do the moving. I still have those lists today. Days, lists, and dozens of confessions of wrongdoing later, my child finally confessed the one lie I knew for sure; it was *last* on the piece of paper—it was a nothing lie. However, on that same piece of paper was the lie that I really wanted to know about—the biggie. It was not at the top of the list or at the bottom. It was strategically buried right in the middle. I do believe that the child instinctively knew that the biggie was the one lie I was really looking for, and so she tried, as best she could, to hide it still. A lot of chaos came to an end that day because I let God do the moving, and patience and time fight the battle for me.

Patience *circumvented sorrow.*

DEVELOPING PATIENCE

"The two most powerful warriors are patience and time."

—Leo Tolstoy

There are lots of reasons why a mom can lose her patience. If we try to become aware of why we lose it, we may be able to take preventative action, overcome impatience, and exercise more patience. So here are the top five reasons why most of us lose our patience, and five ways to build our patience.

Five Reasons Why We Lose Our Patience

1. *Fatigue.* We quickly come to the end of our ropes when we have too much to do and too little energy with which to do it. Add to this the fact that kids seem to have a limitless amount of energy, and you're already tired when you wake up in the morning.

2. *Displaced anger.* Often we are irritated at someone else or about something that has little or nothing to do with the crisis of the moment. Unfortunately, our kids are the easiest, most accessible targets of this displaced anger, and it shows up in impatience with them.

3. *Unrealistic expectations.* We have an agenda that does not take into account the unpredictability of life in general and parenting in particular. Then when we get behind, the pressure pushes us to impatience with everyone around us, including our children.

4. *Failure to plan.* Many times our frustration and anger are of our own making because we fail to put in the extra effort it takes to prepare us, and our children, for the unique demands of the day. Remember: when you fail to plan, you plan to fail.

5. *Distorted perspective.* We assume it is us against

them and that they are out to get us. We see those little charges as the enemy who has us under siege, almost as if they are purposely trying to annoy us, when instead they are really, most often, just children being children in all their imperfections.

To be passionate moms we each must really exercise and strengthen that patience muscle. It is a brick to build, and build it we must. So here are five simple ways to build patience and counteract those reasons why we lose our patience.

Five Ways to Build Our Patience

1. *Reenergize.* Do your best to rest up when the chance presents itself. Even if your kids don't take naps, institute a quiet time in the afternoon.
2. *Deal with your anger.* Ask yourself, "What am I really angry about?" If you can't take care of it immediately, write down your course of action, and then set it aside until you can deal with it. Pray for a gentle spirit toward your kids, and ask forgiveness if needed.
3. *Have realistic expectations.* Once you have a reality check on your perfectly executed day, calculate how much time, energy, and money it will take to pull it off, and then triple it. Barring a flooded basement or an outbreak of chicken pox, you may come close to meeting your expectations at the end of the day.
4. *Plan, plan, plan.* As you anticipate what you need to prepare for the demands of the day, play "worst

case scenario" and plan accordingly. Lists are incredibly helpful, and sticky notes rule! There is only one thing more time consuming than preparing for your day, and that is trying to repair a day gone astray!

5. *Keep a wide-angle perspective.* Remember: it is our job is to love and train our children. Don't take their goofiness and misbehavior personally. They will one day put aside childish behavior and become adults you can relate to.

THE PASSIONATE MOM MUST BE PATIENT

Patience is crucial for our parenting. As Nehemiah did, we must patiently remind ourselves that if God wants our children to have opportunities, he will present them. We must go about our business doing what we know to be our job and let him reveal the way. This does not mean that we do nothing. We will see in the next chapter that when the opportunity came, Nehemiah had prepared ingeniously. He had prepared as if the task depended on him, but he had prayed as if it depended on God. Then he submitted to God and patiently waited, even though my guess is he had probably been prepared to move months earlier. His patience was rewarded, and we will see that he was given far more than he had planned.

> "The key to everything is patience. You get the chicken by hatching the egg, not by smashing it."
>
> —Arnold Glasgow

God's plan is so much bigger than ours, and so much better. But we must be patient or we will smash our little eggs. And while we are patiently waiting on God, we must prepare for the opportunity we are awaiting . . . just as Nehemiah did.

The Brick	The Mortar
Patience	Tolerance
	Discipline

Preparation

We have come to one of my favorite parts of our story. This is where vision meets opportunity, where man's faith fuses with God's faithfulness, and where the King in heaven stirs a king on earth to do his will—all in a two-minute conversation— all because our friend Nehemiah is prepared. How is that for efficiency? Years of devastation for the Israelites; four months of perceiving, pondering, praying, and patiently waiting for Nehemiah; and two minutes of opportunity with the king, and a plan is set in motion—a plan to surround the people of Israel with a wall of protection and provide them a secure future. They are about to be thrown a flotation device, and they don't even know it.

In the month of Nisan in the twentieth year of King Artaxerxes, when wine was brought for him, I took the

wine and gave it to the king. I had not been sad in his presence before, so the king asked me, "Why does your face look
so sad when you are not ill? This can be nothing but sadness of heart."

I was very much afraid, but I said to the king, "May the
king live forever! Why should my face not look sad when
the city where my ancestors are buried lies in ruins, and its
gates have been destroyed by fire?"

The king said to me, "What is it you want?"

Then I prayed to the God of heaven, and I answered the
king, "If it pleases the king and if your servant has found
favor in his sight, let him send me to the city in Judah where
my ancestors are buried so that I can rebuild it."

Then the king, with the queen sitting beside him, asked
me, "How long will your journey take, and when will you
get back?" It pleased the king to send me; so I set a time.

I also said to him, "If it pleases the king, may I have letters to the governors of Trans-Euphrates, so that they will
provide me safe-conduct until I arrive in Judah? And may
I have a letter to Asaph, keeper of the royal park, so he will
give me timber to make beams for the gates of the citadel by
the temple and for the city wall and for the residence I will
occupy?" And because the gracious hand of my God was on
me, the king granted my requests. So I went to the governors
of Trans-Euphrates and gave them the king's letters. The king
had also sent army officers and cavalry with me. (Neh. 2:1–9)

Nehemiah was prepared for this opportunity. It is for
such a time as this that the bricks in our wall-building pay off.
Perception, pondering, passion, prayer, and patience are the

foundation for being prepared and developing a plan. Without the bricks that come before, it is impossible to prepare and carry out a plan. How can you know what you are preparing *for* if you haven't perceived or pondered or prayed or patiently waited for God?

Four months have passed in our story, and Nehemiah had patiently been waiting for an opportunity. This is not to say that he had been sitting around doing nothing. Quite the contrary, Nehemiah had been preparing. We don't know exactly what he was doing, but based on his response to the opportunity that arose, you can tell he had definitely been considering what he might do and what he would need to do it.

Nehemiah left nothing to chance. Nothing that happened in the way his opportunity surfaced caught him by surprise. Preparation is guaranteed paralysis prevention. When we are unprepared, we panic, and when we panic, we become paralyzed. Nehemiah never panicked. His reaction to the king's unexpected question—"What is it you want?"—was flawless because of preparation that took place long before he heard about his people's plight.

Nehemiah had personally prepared himself for years by becoming a man of integrity without even knowing that one day he would be a pivotal player in safeguarding countless lives. He had made it his business to be the best he could be in everything he did. Then, when his passion gave birth to the desire to provide shelter for his people, he prepared a detailed plan and waited for the opportunity to present. As a mother, your character, your integrity, will play into your parenting for good or for bad. And you will have the opportunity to influence, safeguard, and direct the development of your child. Are you prepared?

Brick #6
Preparation
A Passionate Mom must be prepared with personal integrity and a detailed plan in advance of the opportunity.

We don't want to leave our children to chance.

FOUR WAYS NEHEMIAH HAD PREPARED FOR HIS OPPORTUNITY

In just these six short paragraphs, a plan to provide for thousands of people was born because of one man's preparation and a very short conversation:

Paragraph 1: He Had Built Relationships

Because Nehemiah had developed intimate and important relationships with those around him, the king was able to recognize Nehemiah's sorrow.

Paragraphs 2–4: He Had Built Up Confidence

Because Nehemiah had prayed fervently, God had given him the confidence he would need to succinctly and passionately articulate his request. He was able to explain his people's situation boldly.

Paragraph 5: He Had Gained Favor

Because Nehemiah had been faithful, he had found favor with both the king of Babylon and the King of kings.

Paragraph 6: He Had Crafted a Plan

Because Nehemiah had been planning all along, he was able to reveal a detailed plan to the king to accomplish his purpose of rebuilding Jerusalem's walls.

Let's take a closer look at *relationships, confidence, favor,* and the value of a *plan*:

RELATIONSHIPS

Because Nehemiah had established rapport in the palace, the king—the busy, powerful king—*noticed* Nehemiah's expression. Not only did he notice, but he was so intimate with Nehemiah that he was able to infer three things with assurance from his observation: (1) Nehemiah was sad, (2) he was not ill, and (3) he must therefore be suffering from sadness of the heart. The king and Nehemiah had a close relationship, so close they could read each other's expressions.

Nehemiah was the king's cupbearer. Are you picturing a purple damask–clad, subservient-looking man parading in front of the king, ceremoniously carrying a large, bejeweled goblet? Erase that image, because cupbearer to the king was a noble position of great influence in Nehemiah's day. True, the cupbearer was responsible for ensuring that the king's wine was not poisoned, but the position had evolved beyond the simple tasting of wine. Because of his constant access to the king, the cupbearer acquired influence beyond even that of some military leaders and nobles. In some periods of history, the cupbearer was more like a chief of staff.

The reason for this is obvious—only the most trusted

of servants got the lifesaving job. The king would have to be completely convinced of a servant's loyalty to him alone or risk that the servant could be bribed to allow the king to be poisoned. When convinced of such loyalty, the king would most likely come to appreciate the servant's meticulous care of his life. With few people that he could trust, it is understandable that a king might develop a relationship with the constant and loyal cupbearer.

How in the world did Nehemiah, a foreigner, an exile from a country that had been enslaved, with no connections that we know of, work his way into such an influential position? I do not believe it happened overnight or by chance or because he "knew someone." Nehemiah must have had a proven track record of impeccable service. Nehemiah was in a noble position because he had developed noble character.

Integrity: steadfast adherence to a code of honesty, morality, and reliability

Preparation begins with *relationships*, and relationships begin with *integrity*. Before you can ever hope to build relationships with your children, you must be a mom of integrity. Your kids have to know that you are what you say you are and that you will do what you say you'll do. If they don't *trust* you, then the opportunities you are hoping for as they grow may never appear. Your *integrity* is a powerful bonding agent in the mortar of your wall. It will contribute to holding every brick in place.*

Had Nehemiah not had a reputation for being a man of integrity, and if he had not spent time developing a relationship

---

* James Montgomery Boyce, *Nehemiah*, (Ada, MI: Baker Books, 2006), 15.

with the king, he would not have found favor with him. The opportunity to rebuild Jerusalem's wall may have gone to someone else—or to no one. Certainly, Nehemiah himself would have been unable to help his people. What are *you* doing in your job as mom that will put you in a position to help your children? The reality for your kids is that they may not have anybody else. You are their hope; you are their wall; so you must build relationships—both with them and with all who may impact them—with integrity.

With Whom Do Moms Need to Build Relationships?

First, and most important for a million reasons, moms need like-minded friends. If you are a mom of integrity, you will develop friendships with other moms of integrity. For me, my integrity is rooted in my faith in Christ. Most of my closest friends share that faith. Their like-mindedness has been invaluable to me over years of parenting.

The most evident example of a like-minded friend and a mom of integrity is my friend Jan. Jan lived in my neighborhood, and I met her through her sister, but quite honestly, I don't even remember how she came to begin towing me around the neighborhood on bike rides. I say towing because that is Jan—she just sweeps people up and incorporates them into different aspects of her life—lots of them. It is a gift of hers. I was incorporated into her bike riding.

Jan fascinated me. She multitasked with such fluid organization and energy. She could instruct her four-year-old on training wheels, balance *two* children on her bike—a three-year-old in a seat on her handlebars and a six-month-old in a seat behind her—*and* have a purposeful conversation with me as she pedaled her bike. Soon Jan swept me and my one little self-contained infant into her weekly parade. I was mentored, entertained, inspired, and physically exercised, all in one forty-five-minute bike ride. Now, that is efficiency!

Bike riding led to years of Bible study together. Our husbands became friends, and we all started going to the same church. Twenty years later Jan is still in my life, inspiring me and encouraging me daily as I write this book. Jan is an empty-nester, but her passion for children is stronger than ever. Weekly she leads a small group of new moms in a parenting Bible study, and she also mentors an underprivileged student at our high school. And I am still incorporated into her life too—she just makes her relationships work. We are passionately like-minded, and she inspires me to be a better mom.

Beyond friendships, it is important that we moms have good relationships with all of the people who intersect with our children's lives. They will help you prepare a plan for your child by guiding you with information about your child's development and behavior. Here are some examples of people with whom you should have sound relationships, as well as a few tricks you can use to put yourself in a position to interact with them if you are not overtly social:

- *The parents of your child's friends.* One way to get to know other parents is to offer to drive for the car pool to movies or playdates. Call ahead of time and chat about the arrangements. Then, when you pick up a child, get out of the car, go to the door, and introduce yourself to the parents. Every mother loves to hear compliments about her child, so when you return, let her know if her son or daughter was polite and you will have a friend in her before you know it.

- *Teachers.* Volunteer in the classroom, go to every conference and open house, attend class performances, chaperone on field trips, and join the PTA. Every teacher can use some help and some empathy. One act of kindness or a kind word to a teacher who devotes herself to your child for a year can go a long way.

- *Youth workers.* Scoutmasters and church youth leaders can build confidence in your child outside of school. Get to know them by volunteering to help with trips, events, and food. Again, a little help or a kind word may open the door to a mentoring relationship for your child.

- *Coaches and instructors.* These sacrificial, often volunteer people are always in need of help, and you can learn lots of interesting tidbits about your child tacked onto short conversations about Gatorade, coolers, and car pool caravans. And if you go to practices and games, you can meet the moms of your child's teammates. I have developed many a bleacher friendship with moms after years of sitting on benches together! In fact, we often had so many great conversations that our team would score and we would look up in laughter and say, "Uh-oh—was that your son or mine?" But the relationship was definitely worth missing a shot or two.

The Right Relationships Can Be Lifesaving and Faith-Building

Nehemiah went from the business of protecting one life, the king's, from poison, to protecting thousands of lives, his people's, from enemy attack because of one strong, well-nurtured relationship. Life is all about relationships, and I have experienced the lifesaving care that comes from having them.

When I was in high school, I had a cardiac arrest, and it was determined that I needed a pacemaker. It was a life-giving moment for me. From that point forward I believed that God was real, that there was something he wanted me to do, and that my days were numbered, so I needed to find it and be about it. Years after I received my first pacemaker, it gave out. I had three small children ages five, three, and one. New doctors did new tests and gave me a new diagnosis: they felt that I probably didn't need a pacemaker and put me on steroids instead. I was not the same person.

After a year, I made an appointment with my old doctor in Houston for a second opinion. We flew in for the appointment, but when we got there, we had to see his partner instead, due to an emergency. The partner was rather rushed and told us that if the steroids weren't working, don't take them. Period. So I stopped. I didn't know any better.

It took six days before I felt the effects of not weaning slowly off the steroid. I became really sick. The combined complications from discontinuing the steroid and trying to keep my heart beating regularly were debilitating. By then my children were six, four, and two. Every day I would wake up and think, *I can do this; I can will my body to do this. I will eat simply, I will pace myself, I will pray, and it will be better today.*

It wasn't. Some days would be a little better, but most weren't. I was failing my husband, my children, and myself.

My relationships during that year saved me. My husband fought for me. Firmly convinced that I had been fine with a pacemaker, but not fine without it, he dragged me back to the doctors. When they wouldn't listen, he searched for a doctor who would, and he found one. My friends met a million needs. They drove my two girls to school, took them to ballet and parties and playdates, and encouraged me by saying it was nothing, and that my daughters were a pleasure. I *never* had to ask my friends. They always thought of me, talked among themselves, and made sure that someone had my girls covered for everything. My community—church and school moms—fed my family for a year. I am not exaggerating. My dad and stepmother would come often to help. My dad, who loves to eat, was amazed at the number of meals that appeared on my doorstep every time he was there, even after months.

There were many profound faith-building moments in that year. I visibly saw God use others to meet my needs when I couldn't meet them myself. Sometimes God used people I barely knew. It was so humbling and amazing. It was even miraculous. I could not control my health, my days, or my home, but God could, and he used people to do it. People are an investment with a huge return. There may come a day when the people with whom you have relationships will save your life or the life of your child. Or you may have the opportunity to serve them in a way that is lifesaving to them.

---- **Confession** ----

I have said it before, but this book is more for me than anyone else. I am fighting tears of conviction as I write this. I have not been a good friend lately. I have been too busy. Three days after both my husband and I signed book contracts, our house flooded. It was not a water heater flood. It was a getting-a-new-roof-and-tornado-storm-hits-out-of-nowhere flood. Water literally poured into every inch of my house for four hours. One year later and we are still not home. But no excuses. Relationships come first. Always. I know this. In my final minutes of life, I will *not* be thinking of my house. My mind will flash, with a pang to my heart, to the people I love—not the stuff.

The Wrong Kinds of Relationships Can Corrupt Character

"A wife of noble character who can find?" says Proverbs 31:10. "She is worth far more than rubies." I want to be that woman—a wife and mother of noble character. Nehemiah had noble character, and it earned him a position of influence, something he would need.

As a mom I need to have influence over my children, and influence is earned through character. We can read all the parenting books we want. We can get our kids into the best schools, dress them in the priciest clothes, and feed them the healthiest food, but if we do it all without modeling character, it will be ineffective. As we build our walls, character is the mortar that holds the bricks together.

So what does it look like when someone *lacks* character, and what does that have to do with relationships? Let me give you an example.

When my son was still fairly young, he loved baseball. Because he was a good athlete, he was given the opportunity to play in a more serious league. We knew it was a bigger commitment and more competitive situation, but several of his friends would make the move with him. He loved the game and the kids, so it seemed like a good opportunity.

It wasn't. The team worked very hard and was very successful on the scoreboard. But the season was painful, humiliating, and intimidating.

The coach was very smart. He knew exactly what drills and skills were necessary for the players to achieve success. But he totally lacked character, and because of it, his methods where shameful. He called his players names, yelled at them, and humiliated them so that they played out of fear. He coached without humility, self-control, and love, and needless to say, his relationships with his players, not to mention other teams and coaches, were strained. My son completed the season and never played baseball again. There was nothing noble in that season for him, even though they had accomplished the goal of winning.

Our culture doesn't teach character anymore. And so we see hours of reality TV filled with individuals devoid of character. It is not pretty, and it can be very harmful to our children's character. If we are not careful, we will raise children with the same lack of character that we have exposed them to both on TV and in those other overly competitive situations, like my son's baseball team. I am concerned that we get so caught up in what we think our children need to do that we sacrifice our values for the sake of "success." Our kids will soon come to believe that success at any cost is worth more than character, and it will affect their relationships, both now and in the future. In the end, this will to *win* will become a *loss*.

Exercising parenting influence over what type of people you expose your child to will take some pondering. Sometimes you may simply need to remove your child from an unhealthy relationship. Other times it is difficult to move a child, and he or she must instead learn to patiently endure a leader who lacks character. (It is easier to change coaches, for example, than teachers.) But if your child *must* be subjected to lengthy exposure to people without character, be on alert so you can protect him and train him through the experience.

But remember this: character is as much "caught" as it is taught. If you've had children for any length of time, you know that it doesn't matter what you *say*—your child will do what you *do*. If the saying and the doing don't match, the doing will win! I'd like to think Nehemiah "caught" his noble character from parents of noble character—and, of course, from his mom in particular.

What kind of character are your children catching from you?

CONFIDENCE

I love the part of Nehemiah's story where he confidently makes his request of the king! It is the perfect picture of heaven and earth coming into alignment in preparation for some great work.

Nehemiah's desires were in alignment with God's will. God wanted Nehemiah to rebuild the walls of Jerusalem to protect his people, and Nehemiah was willing to do it. The only thing standing in the way was a very powerful, ruthless king. But that was not a problem for God; he is the King of kings. Nehemiah knew this. The knowledge that God can do anything gave Nehemiah confidence. It made him bold. Now read and learn from the strategy of this man—he was a master of diplomacy.

First, he was so human—remember that he said he was *very much* afraid (Neh. 2:2). And he had reason to be afraid of the tyrannical king he served every day. But that didn't stop him. He began his plea with deference, "May the king live forever!" (v. 3). Then he simply stated, succinctly and without political implications, his personal grief over his people's plight. I do not think Nehemiah's opening statement was by accident. He needed to assert his loyalty to the king. He also needed to avoid the politics of why his people were in their situation, as it could have offended the king and made him defensive. Nehemiah had thought it out. He presented the problem from a position of personal grief, not political outrage. Nehemiah did not get caught up with who was to blame for the situation and how to seek justice; he just wanted to move forward and make his people secure.

The effect of Nehemiah's strategy was that the king became sympathetic. His concern and care for the faithful servant suffering before him diverted his thoughts from the political implications of the Israelites' situation. Moved to help Nehemiah, the king asked, "What is it you want?" (v. 4).

The next verse tells us that before Nehemiah uttered a word in response, he prayed to the God of heaven. Can you feel the earth move as it aligns with heaven? Faith can move a mountain, and Nehemiah's utter dependence on and faith in God was about to move *his* mountain, the king. Nehemiah boldly asked for the impossible, with ingenious deference:

"If it pleases the king [in other words, 'because you are king, and your needs come first'] and if your servant has found favor in his sight [that is, 'if I have done a good job'], let him send me to the city in Judah where my ancestors are buried so that I can rebuild it" (v. 5). He wanted to serve the ones he loved in the same faithful way he had served the king.

Nehemiah was so prepared for this opportunity. He had carefully weighed his words well in advance. He took his passion and wisely contained it in a few succinct statements. In manner and in speech he was bold, but with deference. We would be wise to follow his example. Boldness is a character element that will serve your child well as you speak with others on his or her behalf—if it is seasoned with prayer and deference. The prayer is like a check and balance that you cannot skip. It will check your heart for motives, like pride or vengeance, and it will balance your passion with deference and respect. If you pass the check and balance, then you will have confidence that your words and actions are coming from a heart with pure intentions.

Boldness: the ability to confidently go forward, knowing that you have prayed and are prepared

Nehemiah had confidence. And preparation and prayer paved the way to his boldness.

Have you ever had a child stress out over a test? One of our children often melted down before tests. She would become overwhelmed by what seemed like an insurmountable amount of information to study. After much prayer and coaxing, the tears would stop. We would then take out a paper and pen and make a study plan, breaking down the content into manageable pieces. As the child prepared by working through the plan, her confidence would grow. The morning of the test, though there was still some fear, she would boldly go to school, ready for the exam and confident that she would do well.

If the King of kings popped in totally out of the blue for coffee today and casually asked you, "What do want for your child?" what would you say? Do you know what you want? Are you prepared with a plan for your child? Have you prayed enough to be able to answer with confidence, knowing that what you want for your child appropriately aligns with God's will for your child?

FAVOR

"Then the king, with the queen sitting beside him, asked me, 'How long will your journey take, and when will you get back?' It pleased the king to send me; so I set a time."

—Nehemiah 2:6

I think it is so interesting that we get to know that the queen was there too! It lets our imagination explore a little more. Did the king and queen have a little chat? Did she weigh in on the subject? Had Nehemiah found favor with her too? It is all so intriguing. Nehemiah made it look so easy, but we know this was an intense moment before a king who, if angered, would have thought nothing of cutting Nehemiah's throat. His heart was pounding; his adrenaline was pumping. Nehemiah had *worked* for this moment. He had earned this opportunity, and God opened the door for his faithful servant—so that it *pleased* the king (and the queen) to let him go!

My favorite Bible verse says, "I know your deeds. See, I have placed before you an open door that no one can shut. I know that you have little strength, yet you have kept my word and have not denied my name" (Rev. 3:8).

Nehemiah's "deeds" were faithful, so he found favor with the *king*.

Nehemiah kept God's word and did not deny his name, so he found favor with the *King* of kings. Nehemiah gained the favor of two kings: his earthly king and his heavenly King.

Trustworthiness: ability to be trusted or depended on; reliability

Nehemiah was prepared in all things for everyone that counted, and that is why he found favor. Nehemiah was trustworthy.

Can your children rely on you? Oh, you may be thinking, *Of course! I would do anything for my children.* But I am not talking about emergencies. Any mom can see a major red flag and jump on it. I think the king found Nehemiah trustworthy because he was faithful in the little things. He was quietly perceiving, pondering, and praying about what the king would need long before he was asked to provide it.

Children are young, and each is emotionally, intellectually, and socially a work in process. They can't always understand or express their needs, hurts, confusion, and the questions they should ask to find solutions. Sometimes they rely on us for answers and direction to questions they haven't even thought to ask. We can only provide that guidance if we are patiently, perceptively pondering them and their lives.

Nehemiah was worthy of the trust the king had in him, so he found favor. Are you worthy of the same trust? God has given you an opportunity—an open door, Revelation 3 calls it—to raise your children. Can he trust you to train them in the way they should go? *If so, you will find favor with God.*

My husband is very faithful to God, and his greatest desire is to please him. He is also a natural favor finder. He often takes time to help others, and enjoys it. As a result, as our children have grown and needed a part-time job or recommendation, people my husband has helped were pleased to help him and our family in return, even though we didn't expect it. By diligently doing his job and caring for others, my husband is preparing the way to help those he treasures most, our children.

Three Ways You Can Find Favor

Nehemiah had prepared himself for his role in middle management. We have seen that he knew how to work well with those over him—namely, the king. In the chapters to come, we will see that he also knew how to work well with those under his management.

As a mom, have you not felt like a middle manager? You are your child's supervisor, and while you don't report to teachers, coaches, or doctors, you must be the advocate for your child. Nehemiah's diplomacy with the king opened the door to a much-needed opportunity for his people. You can do the same for your child. Think about Nehemiah's winsome approach and how that same approach might help you find favor for your child at your next parent-teacher conference! Here are three things I found in his example. Do as he did and you will find favor.

1. *He was respectful.* Persian kings were absolute rulers and often cruel. Nehemiah may not have agreed with his king, but he respected his position and showed deference. On several occasions in my children's school experiences, they had a teacher or a coach whose philosophy I opposed. In a couple of cases it made for a difficult year. One of our daughters is very fearful of negative attention. She had a teacher who was very harsh and sarcastic. After several conversations with the teacher, I realized she was not empathetic. My only recourse for that year was to encourage my daughter to respect the teacher for her position, pray for favor, and be brave for that one hour every day.

2. *He was tactful.* Nehemiah could have taken this opportunity to really speak his mind, complaining about how the king had stopped the rebuilding of the wall at the request of some other guy who was jealous of the Israelites without ever listening to their side. It does feel good to vent; however, when we do, it usually makes us sound arrogant and angry and it puts the other person on the defensive. I know because I like to vent. It never works in my favor.

   This is what it might look like when you vent using a parent-teacher conference example: The teacher gives a really hard test. Everyone does poorly. You are mad because you think it was unfair to your child. What you don't know, of course, is what has been going on in the class. You begin the conference by letting the teacher know what you think about the test and how unfair it was. The teacher, who may have had a plan or purpose for the test, is now on the defensive and may be mad because you are intimating that she does not know what she is doing. The teacher feels you have misjudged her and refuses to waste her time explaining to you what she planned to do about the test. Hopefully she does not transfer her anger toward you to your child.

Nehemiah did not vent; he simply told the king he was sad because his people were in danger. The king understood and was sympathetic. Using his approach in our teacher example, you could say, "I am very concerned about Megan's grade and would appreciate your advice about what she needs to do to improve it." The teacher in this case is not being blamed and may confess that she did make it hard, or perhaps she may give you some insight into her strategy with this class.

3. *He was careful.* Nehemiah did not launch into a convoluted list that would no doubt leave a busy listener annoyed. He cut right to the heart of the matter—he was sad for his people. If you present a teacher or coach a laundry list of things you think need to change every time you see them, you will not see them much—they will avoid you. Nehemiah earned the right to be heard and carefully saved it for when he really needed it.

THE PLAN

Nehemiah may have been afraid with his first words to the king, but he didn't seem to be afraid. He laid out his intentions with the detail of an experienced building contractor, and yet we know he was not one. But he had done his homework and was prepared to present as much as he could of the details of his plan.

> I also said to him, "If it pleases the king, may I have letters to the governors of Trans-Euphrates, so that they will provide me safe-conduct until I arrive in Judah? And may I have a letter to Asaph, keeper of the royal park, so he will give me timber to make beams for the gates of the citadel by the temple and for the city wall and for the residence I will occupy?" And because the gracious hand of my God was on me, the king granted my requests. So I went to the governors of Trans-Euphrates and gave them the king's letters. The king had also sent army officers and cavalry with me. (Neh. 2:7–9)

And that was that. Months of preparation, and with a single two-minute conversation, a plan to safeguard a nation was born. Preparation and prayer. Remember how Nehemiah began this adventure with a prayer? He ended that prayer with one request: "Give your servant success today by granting him favor in the presence of this man [the king]" (Neh. 1:11).

His prayer was answered, and now he could execute his plan.

THE PASSIONATE MOM MUST BE PREPARED

The passionate mom must patiently prepare. She must develop relationships with the people in her life and her child's life. She must build up her confidence through prayer so she can succinctly and passionately articulate her requests on her child's behalf when presented with an opportunity. She must gain the favor of God and others by being faithful and trustworthy. And she must carefully craft a plan to accomplish her purpose for her child.

Do you pray that you and your child will find favor with his teacher? coach? How about friends? How about the crabby neighbor down the street who doesn't like children? The reward for such diligent preparation is the joy of knowing you have contributed well to providing your child with a future. Nehemiah's preparation certainly contributed well to providing his people with a safe, secure future.

The next brick we need to add to the wall is a biggie—purpose. Without a clearly defined purpose, a mom can flounder, a child can flounder, and life can get very unclear. Nehemiah had a clear understanding of his purpose. We should too.

The Brick	The Mortar
Preparation	Integrity
	Boldness
	Trustworthiness

Purpose

The king said to me, "What is it you want?"
—Nehemiah 2:4

When the king realized that his cupbearer wanted something from him, he asked him a question, and Nehemiah answered—emphatically and without hesitation. Nehemiah had a purpose, and he was passionate about it. Perhaps, in that second suspended in the air between the king's question and Nehemiah's answer, a small battle waged unseen.

You see, Nehemiah had a choice. He could play it safe and save himself, or he could be obedient to God and build a wall that would save his people from disgrace. Remember: to display emotion or express an opinion, let alone make a request, unsolicited to the king, could result in a death sentence, especially if the king felt the request had political implications, which it did, in this case.

Nehemiah made the right choice—he risked his life to please his God. I don't think it was a difficult choice for him.

He passionately loved God and his people. Nehemiah knew that God had placed him in his position, and he was determined to fulfill his purpose: to guarantee the future of Israel. We will see in coming chapters that in many ways the Israelites were like his children (there is no record that he had children of his own or a wife) and his passion and purpose were similar to a mom's.

If you have been blessed with children, then as a mom, you should have a purpose for your parenting. But what other purposes do you have? On any given day of your life what "want" is a priority to you? What occupies your thoughts and time? Do you want a new couch? A new car? A bigger house? A better husband? Smarter kids? What do you spend your time looking at, reading about, or doing? If we are passionate about our children, then our purpose *as parents* should be what is uppermost on our minds. What are you parenting for? All A's on the next report card? The first seat in the orchestra? A baseball scholarship? Is that your vision? If we are pondering and praying, we will come to a conclusion about our purpose and know exactly what we want to accomplish as moms.

Confession

If I were asked on any given day what it is that I want most, my answer would vary. I confess that "my life's purpose" would not be at the top of the list of what might pop out of my mouth. I am often preoccupied by the material things I want and the tasks I need to get done right now. And that preoccupation can rob my focus from what is really important in life.

"Susan, what is it you want?"

I really believe that my King, God, asks me that every day. Unfortunately, I am not always prepared, as Nehemiah was. Most often my desires are just that—*my* desires—and they are not in alignment with God's desires for me. This side of heaven, I cannot know how many opportunities I have missed as a mom because I did not pray and realign my desires. This saddens me, because those missed opportunities may affect my family as well.

Are you moving so fast through life that you really don't have a clear picture of your purpose? When we do not take the time to ponder and pray about our purpose and what God wants for us, we can end up falling short of our goal. The lack of focus on our purpose will reveal itself in missed opportunities at some point, and the passionate mom will feel the regret quite passionately.

Brick #7
Purpose
A Passionate Mom knows the reason for her existence as a parent and is determined to fulfill it.

What is it you want? How do you determine what to want for your parenting? Are you making plans of your own, or are you allowing God to be involved and to direct you in your purpose for parenting?

HOW TO DETERMINE YOUR PURPOSE IN PARENTING

How does one come up with a purpose? Well, first recognize that you can have more than one purpose. Certainly Nehemiah had a purpose with regard to his faith and his relationship with God. I am sure he also had a purpose for his work. Then he developed a purpose to save his people from disgrace and rebuild the walls of their city. You can have a purpose for your faith, your family, your work, and anything else you have a passion for.

We will be focusing on finding your purpose as a mom. But we won't be taking a typical "mom" approach. I do not have expertise in family psychology or early childhood development. My expertise is in the corporate sector. My mother was an accountant, and my dad was a banker. I was a finance major, a corporate lending officer, and a regional marketing manager. So I easily relate to Nehemiah's businesslike approach, and I think it is an approach that can bring a lot of clarity to a mom trying to define her purpose and her goals for her children. I have found that it makes perfect sense to apply the strategic principles of business to parenting. Is that not what Nehemiah did? He took his people's personal dilemma and applied his well-developed business acumen, acquired from service in the palace, to accomplish God's will. We are intelligent moms; can we not do the same in our parenting?

Jim Collins, author of *Good to Great* and *Built to Last*, has studied and written much about many of America's most successful corporations and what made them so great. As you read what he discovered in his research, think about how you could apply what Jim says about companies to the family.

> Build your company around a core ideology.
> In 17 of the 18 pairs of companies in our research, we found the visionary company was guided more by a core ideology—core values and a sense of purpose beyond just making money—than the comparison company was. A deeply held core ideology gives a company both a strong sense of identity and a thread of continuity that holds the organization together in the face of change.
> We chose the word *ideology* because we found an almost religious fervor in the visionary companies as they grew up that we did not see to the same degree in the comparison companies. 3M's dedication to innovation, P&G's commitment to product excellence, Nordstrom's ideal of heroic customer service, HP's belief in respect for the individual—those were sacred tenets, to be pursued zealously and preserved as a guiding force for generations.

Collins goes on to explain how to use core values with a drive for progress to achieve what he calls Big Hairy Audacious Goals (BHAG).

> Stimulate progress through BHAGs . . .
> To build a visionary company, you need to counterbalance its fixed core ideology with a relentless drive for progress. While core ideology provides continuity, stability, and cohesion, the drive for progress promotes change, improvement, innovation, and renewal.

One way to bring that drive for progress to life is through BHAGs (short for Big Hairy Audacious Goals) . . . The point is not to find the "right" BHAGs but to create BHAGs so clear, compelling, and imaginative that they fuel progress.*

A true BHAG, by definition "is clear and compelling, serves as unifying focal point of effort, and acts as a clear catalyst for *team spirit*. It has a clear finish line, so the organization can know when it has achieved the goal; people like to shoot for finish lines."**

Nehemiah was guided by a core ideology—faith in God as defined by Judaism. Nehemiah's deeply held core ideology gave the Israelites the strong sense of identity and thread of continuity they needed to rally together. And tied to his core belief was his BHAG—his people needed the temple to maintain a relationship with God; both the temple and the people needed to be protected by the wall. Therefore, Nehemiah's purpose was to rebuild the wall and protect the temple and his people from any threat. Because Nehemiah had a clearly defined BHAG, his purpose was clearly defined and compelling and easily provided a catalyst for the Israelites.

I believe that visionary moms are guided by core values and a sense of purpose beyond just worldly success. Their deeply held core ideology gives their families a strong sense of identity and a thread of continuity that holds them together in the

---

* Jim Collins, "Building Companies to Last," *Inc.*, Special Issue: "The State of Small Business," 1995, http://www.jimcollins.com/article_topics/articles/building-companies.html.

** Collins, J. & Porras, J., *Building Your Company's Vision*, Vol. 74, Iss. 5: Harvard Business Review (1996), 65–77.

face of change and even trials and tribulations. If a mom wants to drive for progress in her parenting, she needs to know her purpose and how to hit that clearly defined target that she is shooting for. What is it that you want? What is your goal? Define it and you will have your purpose for parenting. To help us find our purpose, we need to answer these questions:

- What are your core beliefs?
- What is your goal for your children?
- What is your purpose as a mother, and how will you work it to reach your goal?

Every mom will answer these questions differently. And that is what makes life so exciting. We are all unique, with unique perspectives, unique children, and unique opportunities. Through pondering and prayer you will find your values and define your purpose. My core values and goal, like Nehemiah's, are only examples for you. This is how I answered:

- What are your core beliefs?
    My core belief is a belief in God. I believe that his Son, Jesus Christ, died for the forgiveness of my sins and my salvation.

- What is your goal for your children?
    My goal is for my children to have a faith of their own when they are ready to leave home.

- What is your purpose as a mother, and how will you work it to reach your goal?

> I will train my children so that they grow in
> wisdom, stature, and favor with God and man.

Because God is central in my core beliefs, I determined that my goal—what I wanted for my children—was for each to have a faith strong enough so that once they left me, God would still be able to direct them long after they had grown. It is what I call my umbrella theory. God is my umbrella; I am my kids' umbrella, and he placed them for a time under the protection of my umbrella. As they grow, they venture out from under my umbrella. When they do, I tell them, "I cannot protect you; you are under God's umbrella now, so make sure you obey him."

As young adults, they will permanently leave the haven of my umbrella. If they have a relationship with God, he will be their umbrella and will direct them. To accomplish my purpose, I determined that I would focus on the four benchmarks that are mentioned with respect to Christ's growing-up years in Luke 2:52: "Jesus grew in wisdom and stature, and in favor with God and man." Because my core beliefs are centered in Christ, I figured that if these were the ways Jesus grew, then they would be the best ways for my children to grow.

PASSION + PURPOSE = A PLAN

These three bricks—passion, purpose, and planning—have a special relationship that can make or break a wall. And, of course, it all starts with passion. Without passion you won't have the drive to develop a purpose, and if you don't ever find a purpose, you surely won't see the need to have a plan.

In my example of defining my purpose, this is how the bricks of passion, purpose, and planning came together:

My Passion:	*my children*

+

My Purpose:	*training my children to have a faith of their own when they are ready to leave home*

=

My Plan:	*focus on their growth in wisdom, stature, and favor with God and man*

You cannot move on to the plan until you have nailed down your purpose.

FOCUS YOUR PASSION

Nehemiah had a very narrow focus for his passion—God and the Israelite people. And I can relate. I was exposed to eternity for just a breath of time when my heart stopped, but everything that I loved had time to flash through my mind. God and the people I love: that is all I saw. When your heart stops, your mind will freeze where your heart left off—with those you love.

I don't really believe you can "love" stuff—houses, careers, money. You may desire it. You may think you love it, but that is your eye trying to trick your heart. When your heart stops, your eyes will close, and what you really love will be as clear as day. That is your real passion.

Nehemiah had passion, and he applied it to his vision and developed a purpose—to protect his people from all harm. Then he added more passion to his purpose and came up with a plan. He refused to be distracted, frightened, or discouraged from the plan to fulfill his purpose. There was opposition, lots of it, and it was not easy, but we will see in chapter 10 that because Nehemiah had focused passion, he was undeterred and overcame all obstacles.

FIX YOUR PURPOSE

Nehemiah fixed his purpose—he knew exactly what he needed to do. You have to know your target before you shoot. What are you shooting your child toward? Could it be that failure to launch in young adults is a phenomenon because they never had a target? We must focus our passion and fix our purpose—so what is your BHAG for your child?

It takes great determination to focus your passion and fix your purpose for the duration of your child's maturation. Unfortunately, there are so many beautiful, fascinating, and downright cool things to take our eyes off what we love. Also, I know many of you not only parent but work and serve others. Your time is limited, and your energy wanes at times, but with determination mixed into the mortar of your wall, you can fix your purpose.

I believe that every mother has passion for her child. Some moms have been distracted from their passion; some are sick or weary and their passion is drained low, but it is in there somewhere. But do we all have a vision of where that passion can carry us, a BHAG for our child that is so big and intimidating that it is impossible without God? I think we need more moms to ponder, to pray, to catch a vision for their children, to add in more passion and turn the vision into a purpose; then and only then can we turn our purpose into a plan.

Determination: the act of coming to a decision or of fixing a purpose

> *"If the size of the vision for your life is not intimidating to you, then there is a good chance it is insulting to God."*
>
> —Steven Furtick

THE PASSIONATE MOM MUST HAVE PURPOSE

As a mom, if you are passionate about your children, then you must have a purpose for your parenting. What core values would you like to instill in your child? What goal would you like to reach as a parent? If you can answer these questions, you can define your purpose—the reason you exist as a parent—and you can determine to fulfill it.

Nehemiah was ready to pursue his life purpose; it was the goal toward which he would relentlessly drive himself. It was a vision of what he had been called to do, and it was enormous and more than anything he probably ever saw himself doing. We will see in the coming chapters that he was bold, strategic, and undeterred, and yet he was winsome and fair. He was not a tyrannical leader but a noble leader, one you would be proud to follow. And follow him we can, because he *knew* where he was going. You cannot lead unless you know where you are going. You have to know your purpose.

Find *your* purpose. Then and only then, with the target of where you are going clearly in sight, can you begin the plan for your children. A plan with a Big Harry Audacious Goal. A plan that has a purpose bigger than we are. A plan that dares to parent in today's world.

The Brick	The Mortar
Purpose	Determination

Planning

Finally—we get to the *plan*! If you are an action girl, like me, you have been waiting for the takeaway. So let's start planning!

Hopefully, in the previous chapter you thought about your goals for your child and discovered your purpose for parenting. Now all you need is to cook up a plan. Nehemiah, man of action that he was, had definitely cooked up a plan. Thoughts of the wall and the risk to his people had deeply stirred his passion. He could not let go of the news about them. To his passion he added the yeast of pondering and praying and mixed it all together. The yeast infused and expanded his passion to three times its prior volume. Only prayer and pondering can do that.

By the time the king asked him about the sadness on his face, four months had passed, and Nehemiah's passion had been baked into a golden delicious purpose for his life. He was going to rebuild Jerusalem's wall to shield his people. His purpose permeated every thought in his mind until a plan began to develop. With his plan pressed firmly into his mind and his passion on fire in his heart, Nehemiah answered the king and put his plan into action. He was about to deliver his plan to his people as he'd serve them a loaf of freshly baked bread, the kind that provides nourishment, warmth, safety—life.

I want to do that for my children more than anything. I want to have a plan that will provide them life—nourishment, warmth, safety—for this life and for eternity. Remember: Ezra came before Nehemiah and built the temple and the people's relationship with God. Nehemiah built the wall to protect that temple and that relationship. Protection and preparation in this life mean nothing if there is no hope for eternity.

WHY YOU NEED A PLAN

If I had been Nehemiah, at this point I would probably have thrown up. It is one thing to ponder and pray about traveling to another country to basically take over and whip an entire nation into action; it is another to have the king smile, open the door to his treasury, and say, "Go for it." When you get confirmation of your prayers with a miracle of this magnitude, you know God is on the move, and he wants you to do something big. What an honor this was, but I would have had a lot of trepidation at the enormity of the responsibility.

Nehemiah didn't even know these people—had probably never been to Jerusalem. He couldn't send a mass e-mail and tell them he was on his way; he couldn't access Google Earth and survey the situation from his laptop. He had the plan to go, but he surely didn't know all that it would entail. There was a lot of uncertainty. This was a big, bold plan that was way beyond his ability—way beyond anyone's ability but God's.

Is not parenting the same? You dream and pray about having sweet little pea-pops. You fantasize about all the fun you will have as they grow. Then you deliver or adopt and you feel that little life wiggle in your arms for the very first time. The realization dawns on you that *this is a miracle*, and you know with deep conviction that God is on the move and wants you to do something really scary and big—raise this fragile, precious child.

You feel such honor that you have been chosen, but you are so passionate about this little one that the responsibility is overwhelming. You know you *cannot* mess up, but the uncertainty of what, exactly, parenting your child will require is looming in front of you. There is no software that allows you to map out the perfect parenting path to take with your child. Each infant is uncharted territory. You must have a plan, like the courageous Nehemiah.

There are times—many times, in my case—during seasons of immeasurable exhaustion, when it feels that your plan is way beyond your ability. It takes great courage to face the unknown, and there are many unknowns in parenting. Sometimes we moms have to go to places we never wanted to go. I know a mom who has spent hours in cancer hospitals. I know a mom who flew from Tampa to San Francisco and lived there for months so her unborn child would have the specialist care he needed to survive. Another mom manages hours of a daily medical regimen that includes tube feeding, annual surgery, and patient love for a child who can't talk or walk and never will. And four moms with whom I'm acquainted went through the valley of death with their children and returned empty-handed. There is great joy in parenting those little pea-pops, but there are also frightening unknowns that require courage.

No matter where your parenting path takes you, you must know that you would not have been given the privilege if you were not up to the responsibility. And that responsibility includes having a plan for the life of your child. Without a plan you are leaving your child to chance. According to author and former chairman of Thomas Nelson Publishers Michael Hyatt, few of us have a plan for our own lives. How much less do we plan our children's?

> I have met very few people who have a plan for their lives. Most are passive spectators, watching their lives unfold a day at a time. They may plan their careers, the building of a new home, or even a vacation. But it never occurs to them to plan their life. As a result, many end up discouraged and disillusioned, wondering where they went wrong.*

We could say the same thing about our children's lives:

I have met very few moms who have a plan for their parenting. Most are passive spectators, watching their children's lives unfold a day at a time. They may plan their careers, the building of a new home, or even a vacation. But it never occurs to them to plan their life with their child. As a result, many end up discouraged and disillusioned, wondering where they went wrong as a mom.

---

* Michael Hyatt, *Creating Your Personal Life Plan* (self-published e-book) michaelhyatt.com.

Parenting is a part of your life plan, so you must have a plan, not only for your child's life, but for your life *with* your child. What does it mean to "parent"? The definition of parenting is so simple:

That is a basic plan, but is that all? Food, shots, and a few baths ought to take care of it. And if we threw in daily affection and a collar with an address tag for safety, we could say we have a plan. That may be the definition for *parenting*, but it is not the definition for *mothering*. Being a mom is anything but simple! We can be passive spectators of our dogs, watching their lives unfold one day at a time, but we should not be passive spectators of our children. If you have chosen to be a mom, then parenting must be a big—no, an enormous—part of your life plan.

Parenting: the rearing of a child; to take care of and support a child up to maturity

It should be a passion, and you should have a purpose. You have chosen to invest in the next generation of little people, and there is nothing God cares about more than people. Nehemiah knew this; his people were God's people, and they were at risk. Your children are God's children, and without a plan they, too, could be at risk. Every mom needs a plan. And not just for packing lunches in the morning and folding clothes at night. Every mom needs a long-term, I've-only-got-eighteen-years-with-this-child plan.

Brick #8
The Plan
A Passionate Mom has a plan for parenting her children from birth to adulthood.

THREE STEPS TO A PLAN: A-C-T

Every plan needs a leader. Without a leader nothing gets accomplished. If you have a husband, he is the leader for your family. Bring him in and plan with him. You need to be working on the same plan, and he will bring gifts to the planning that will add to it. Nehemiah was an amazing leader for his people, but he had to go it alone. If you don't have a husband, know that you can lead alone too. A leader is someone people will follow. You are in charge of your children, and with strong mortar and a brick-filled wall, you can lead them. And if Nehemiah could get thousands of strangers to follow him and build a massive wall, certainly I can get my five children to follow me and fold the laundry! We can do this; we just need a plan.

So follow the leader! And Nehemiah is it.

When the time had come for Nehemiah to take action, he had a three-step process to formulate and execute his plan: *Assess, Confirm,* and *Team-build,* or ACT. ACT will work for every mom, even though each will have unique children and a different goal and purpose for parenting. So dig in. Here are the three things you must do to execute your plan.

1. Assess

It pleased the king to send me; so I set a time.

I also said to him, "If it pleases the king, may I have letters to the governors of Trans-Euphrates, so that they will provide me safe-conduct until I arrive in Judah? And may I have a letter to Asaph, keeper of the royal park, so he will give me timber to make beams for the gates of the citadel by the temple and for the city wall and for the residence I will occupy?" And because the gracious hand of my God was on me, the king granted my requests. So I went to the governors of Trans-Euphrates and gave them the king's letters. The king had also sent army officers and cavalry with me. (Neh. 2:6–9)

Assess the Situation

Nehemiah's assessment of Israel's situation was rudimentary at this point. It consisted of figuring out what he thought he would need based upon what he knew. Remember: he probably had never been to Judah. All his information was secondhand. But he did not let the unknown stop him. He pursued his purpose by studying what he could. As a mom you can do the same.

The point of this parenting journey is to look back and be able to say, "I did it. I accomplished what I purposed to accomplish." That does not mean you were perfect or that your child was perfect. It means that as information was revealed to you, you assessed it and made it a part of the plan.

Here is some good news about assessment. It doesn't take a rocket scientist, psychologist, or great theologian. All it takes is the bricks of perceiving and pondering! In fact, a five-year-old can assess with wisdom. Years ago, when my son, Mark, started school, as with his sisters before him, I was anxious for him to make some good friends. At the end of the very first week I received a call from a mom inviting him over for a playdate. *Wonderful!* I thought. *Let's get started making good friends.*

But when I told him about the invitation, all he said was, "No." That's it. I was disconcerted at his decisive, almost disrespectful answer and tried to persuade him to go. Mark was emphatic. Then I became concerned that he was going to be antisocial, and I tried exploring why. He is not a very chatty child, and I acquired no satisfactory information, so I resorted to compromise. I thought maybe he was afraid to go to a stranger's house so I told him we could have the child to our house. He relented, and I called the mother to explain what I thought was my son's shyness.

I picked the boys up from school several days later. Lunch was interesting. The boy would not eat anything offered and demanded bread and butter. My son just stared at me. Then our guest wanted to jump on our trampoline, so out they went.

I was doing dishes when Mark marched in and headed to his room, saying only, "I told you I didn't want to play with him." I asked why, and he said the boy pushed him. I persuaded Mark to go back out and promised I would watch them and talk to the boy if he did it again. Sure enough, he did. So I went out and explained to our guest the trampoline rules, including "No pushing." The whole time, though, Mark was giving me "the look."

I went back inside and watched. I wasn't at the window for ten seconds when the child pushed Mark again. Mark stood up; found my eyes in the window; gave me a long, knowing, exasperated look; turned around; picked the boy up; and threw him down. He then quite calmly climbed through the net of the trampoline, walked across the yard into the house, passed me in the kitchen, and went to his room—without a word. As I said, he is not chatty, *but* he is very perceptive. In

that one week of school, my sweet, insightful son had prop-
erly assessed this child and with wisdom decided he did not
want to play with him. I was clueless! If even a five-year-old
can have the wisdom to know when something that he has
perceived is true, so can a passionate mom.

You can seek wisdom in your parenting and use it to assess
your child's situation.

Assess What You Will Need

The Bible doesn't say that when Nehemiah prayed that
first time he knew exactly how he was going to rebuild the
wall. But we do know that four to five months passed before
the king was moved by Nehemiah's downcast expression to
ask why. In those months, while Nehemiah patiently waited
for his opportunity, he must have used his time wisely to
formulate his plan, because when the king opened the door,
Nehemiah had a detailed list of what he needed. He had obviously spent considerable time assessing so he could provide an
accurate estimate.

The lesson here is that we cannot be afraid to move forward if we don't have all the information. God can lead one
step at a time. Keep your eye on the path before you, and if you
are going to look up, don't let your eyes stop at forest level; look
all the way up to the Director of this show and trust in him. If
that doesn't work, then look back down and hit your knees in
prayer until you can look up again.

Nehemiah may have never seen the city or the wall, but
he still made a list of what he knew he would need: (1) letters
to prove that he was on a mission with the king's permission; and (2) supplies to build the gates, walls, and his own

residence. And then, because God is good and gracious and helps us out in a million ways we don't notice, God moved the king to give Nehemiah something he didn't even ask for: a royal escort of army officers. What a gift, so big that Nehemiah would probably never have asked for it. God knows what we need. If it is our desire to find favor with him, he will make up for our oversights and give us what we need when we need it.

Sometimes we must begin planning before we have all the necessary information. In the meantime, start with your goal. Did you make a goal or recommit to one in the last chapter? With that goal in mind, assess what you know about your child. Then you can start to construct a plan for more than today and tomorrow. You can develop a plan for your child's *life*, and yours!

Assess How to Apply Your Purpose to Your Child

A plan can look a thousand different ways for a thousand different moms, but here is how I tried to keep it a focused goal in my life with five very different little personalities.

My purpose is to do all I can to help my children grow in wisdom, stature, and favor with God and man.

My original goal included four areas that I wanted to watch for each child. I added a fifth.

1. *Wisdom*: my child should be growing in knowledge and making good choices.
2. *Physical*: my child should be growing in size, strength, and health.
3. *Spiritual*: my child should have a faith,

independent of mine, by the time he or she is ready
to leave home.

4. *Relational*: my child should show love for others,
   including family and friends.

5. *Emotional*: my child should understand his or her
   temperament and possess an understanding of self.

The fifth area I assess was an Emily addition. Emily seemed to have a more challenging temperament type that my little predictable firstborn, Megan, did not. So I added "emotional." Emily was very emotional and passionate. I needed to parent her in that area, so I had to put it into my goal. It just didn't fit anywhere else for me. The point is, your plan needs to fit your family, and you know your family best.

When I assessed each of my children, I pondered how they were growing in wisdom, physically, spiritually, relationally, and emotionally. I wanted them to grow in all areas, but as they did, I realized that each had a natural bent in certain areas, and in those they grew naturally. The areas that were less natural to them needed more motivation and encouragement from me.

Following are growth "snapshots" of my two oldest, totally different girls. These are what I call their "floor plans." Each of my children has a different floor plan with different-sized rooms depending on where they like to hang out. The size of the room depicts for me how strong each child is in that area. Megan is rather balanced in four rooms, and her growth in them was steady and predictable. Her fifth room, relational strength, is her gift, and it grew faster because that is where she likes to hang out.

Megan - Age 23

Physical	Wisdom	Relational
swam for 18 years	obedient	loves people
exercises regularly	makes good choices	lots of close friends
eats well	good student	keeps up with everyone
rarely sick	works hard	enjoyed being a swim coach more than swimming
		great babysitter
		chose a large public university
		majored in public relations
Spiritual	**Emotional**	↓
disciplined	age appropriate	currently working for
likes to study	even-tempered	Regions Bank in human
knowledgeable	rational	relations

Megan's natural bent is relational. It was very important to her that she have a good group of friends, and she did, starting at age four. There were four girls, and they swam together on a team, went to church together, did Bible study together, and attended high school together. During their college years, they became separated by distance but remained close and celebrated their senior year by traveling through Europe together.

Megan grew evenly in the other four areas. Her motivation for spiritual and physical growth usually had its root in her desire to be with her friends in Bible studies and sports. Her growth in wisdom and emotion usually stemmed from her desire to please her parents, again a relational motive. My plan was rather easy with her—just keep her motivated relationally in all areas. The result was that Megan grew in every way and—no surprise to us—developed a passion for people. Megan just graduated with a degree in public relations and got a job in human relations. She has a disciplined, relational faith that has made her ready to leave home.

Emily - Age 21

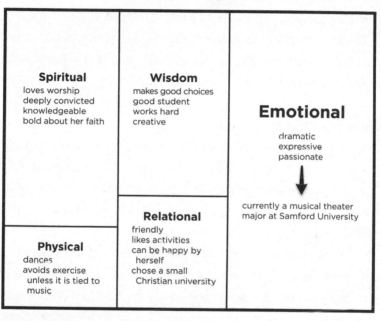

Emily's floor plan is very different from Megan's. Emily's natural bent is emotional. She is motivated by passion. It is very important for Emily to be emotionally involved with what she is doing. Her relationships are very in-the-moment, and she can make friends in a minute, but she doesn't need them to be content. Emily needs to be inspired to be content. Music, creating art, and drama motivate her.

My plan for Emily was a little trickier to accomplish

because a source of motivation was not always readily available. She can only be enticed to exercise if she is moved by music or the romance of the wind blowing through her hair on a bike ride! To motivate Emily to learn the Bible, we used *Adventures in Odyssey* tapes. They dramatically teach Bible stories and biblical principles in audio adventures. She would listen to them for hours.

Her passion can make her impulsive, so self-control was a character quality we had to plan to practice. On the other hand, her faith, fueled by her passion, has made her a bold witness for Christ even in the face of persecution. For Emily, Samford University was a no-brainer—aesthetically, it is the most beautiful campus in the South, its students are filled with a passion for God, and it has a musical theater department. Beauty, passion, and drama—everything that motivates Emily. College has given Emily the opportunity to continue to add discipline to her life in a faith-friendly environment. She will be ready to leave home very soon.

In these examples you are seeing two of my children who are adults now. These are the positives that came out of their maturation process. You are not seeing the struggles and lessons learned to get to this point because if I shared everything about my children, there would be a mutiny in the Merrill home and I would be tossed overboard! But please know that every child has weaknesses, and there will be lessons to learn in all areas. I bring that up because you must manage the temptations and distractions that prey upon your child as a part of the plan too.

My girls are older, so you need to know that by the time your child goes to college, your opportunities for correction are nearly gone. With my sons, who are in high school, these diagrams would each have a plan that involves a lot of correcting, and I can't share that with you because they are still in the process! We will cover how to assess and plan for the gates to independence in the next chapter.

So here are the basics: Determine your goal, if you haven't already. Assess your child. Begin constructing a plan. You may not know exactly what your plan will require, but you can make a list of what you do know and start. Move forward by experimenting with each area of your child's development. As you experiment, assess the results, and then modify your plan as you go. But assess, because if you do that well, you will get where you want to go with your child.

2. Confirm

> I went to Jerusalem, and after staying there three days I set out during the night with a few others. I had not told anyone what my God had put in my heart to do for Jerusalem. There were no mounts with me except the one I was riding on.
>
> By night I went out through the Valley Gate toward the Jackal Well and the Dung Gate, examining the walls of Jerusalem, which had been broken down, and its gates, which had been destroyed by fire. Then I moved on toward the Fountain Gate and the King's Pool, but there was not enough room for my mount to get through; so I went up the valley by night, examining the wall. Finally, I turned back and reentered through the Valley Gate. The officials did not know where I had gone or what I was doing, because as yet I had said nothing to the Jews or the priests or nobles or officials or any others who would be doing the work. (Neh. 2:11–16)

This was a covert operation! And it would require keen discernment on Nehemiah's part. Nehemiah was so discerning. Picture this: Nehemiah rode into town with what must have been an impressive show for the struggling group of Israelites—army officers and cavalry straight from the king. He visited for three days, or at least they probably thought he was just visiting with them, because he told them nothing about why he was there. I think he put them immediately at ease and just let them chatter while he covertly took detailed notes for that ever-evolving plan in his mind. No doubt, he gathered information from old men woefully complaining about needing a new wall, from young men boasting about

Discernment: the keen ability to correctly judge

their dreams beyond the wall, and from women gossiping about scandal within the walls. Then, after he had heard all he needed to hear about the wall, he set out to see the wall for himself. Nehemiah was appropriately sneaky! But *as* he sneaked, he used his well-honed power of *discernment* to separate fact from fiction so he could correctly judge the depth of his challenge and the strategy required to address it.

To confirm your parenting strategy, Nehemiah-style, you are *also* going to need discernment.

A passionate mom must have keen judgment to gather and confirm information about her child.

Confirm Your Strategy

Nehemiah was such a man of intrigue, and I love that he didn't mind telling us about his secrecy. He had a God-given job to do, and he was not concerned that the Israelites might think it was an invasion of privacy. He reported that he and a few others circled the wall, at night, when no one would see him, and he didn't tell anyone else he was going. Nehemiah was not ashamed or of the mind-set that there was anything politically incorrect with being appropriately secretive. Go Nehemiah!

There are five lessons to be learned here that will give you courage for your own mission.

1. *Sometimes covert is the way to go.* Nehemiah never told anyone why he was in Jerusalem. He did not feel obligated to give information to his people. Neither should you. His plan was still in development. Nehemiah, *the leader,* knew that a plan well formed would be well received. Had he opened up discussion with only half-formed ideas and understanding, the city's inhabitants may have lost confidence in his ability to lead them. He may also have made enemies if he rejected any suggestions they made. Offensively, as a leader, if you don't know enough, you may not be effective in persuading others to follow. People, even children, want to know they are following someone who knows where he or she is going. Defensively, if you react too quickly, without accessing the necessary facts, your children will know that you don't really know the score. That may tempt them to pretend they don't know what you are talking about or tell you lies to get out of trouble. You are the mom, the leader, and you do not have to tell your children everything. You spend a lot of time wondering what

they are up to, so it is okay for them to occasionally wonder what you are doing.

2. *Listening is vital.* Nehemiah listened for *three days.* He was gifted at making others feel comfortable. He was also good at finding favor—he must have graciously put his people at ease just as he done with the king. I would guess that the more comfortable the people got, the more they talked, and the more they talked, the more information Nehemiah could gather, until he had a good picture of how the people perceived their situation. My favorite place to listen is in the car. I like to volunteer to drive my kids and their friends anywhere. I just put them at ease with a greeting and a little friendly banter when they get in the car, put on some good tunes, and listen to them go—chatter, chatter. They forget I am there! Fabulous information surfaces. Personalities come out, school happenings are discussed, and interests are explored. I love getting to know other kids and seeing how my kids relate to others.

3. *You need to see things with your* own *eyes.* Nehemiah knew that a picture is worth a thousand words, but no one can give him that picture. He had to get that picture with his own eyes to gain an accurate understanding. He personally inspected the wall, alone. You almost get the feeling that after three days of listening, he was still looking for some missing pieces of information. Or maybe he was getting conflicting information and needed to verify it.

This is where we sense he was nearing some conclusions. As a mom, you must access information firsthand to confirm your strategy before you take action.

Confession

I have jumped to conclusions based on the observations of others, with very bad results. A mom once called me to report an offense that had occurred with a group of children on a playdate. She implied that my child had played a large part. I reacted in haste and jumped on my daughter, only to find in the end that what actually happened was quite the contrary. Another friend confirmed that she had witnessed my daughter actually trying to intervene and rectify the offense. I really hurt my daughter by failing to get all the facts and by believing my friend over her.

4. *You needn't ask permission.* Nehemiah did not ask the people's permission to survey the wall. God gave him the responsibility, so he figured it was his job, and that he alone was responsible. You are responsible for your children. You do not have to ask their permission to access information about them. If you know one of your kids is in trouble, as Nehemiah knew his people were in trouble, then you have all the permission you need to circle your son or daughter, without telling that child—or anyone

else. In short, do anything you can to become aware of the details of your children's troublesome activities. Perhaps you're asking, "Should I read their text messages?" Well, do you pay for the phone? Or "should I monitor their computer activity?" Is the computer in your house? Your child, the phone, and the computer in your house are all your responsibility. It is your job to manage them. If you don't guide and protect your child from the activity that transpires on your property, who will? (More thoughts and details on the complications of parenting well in an age of technology will be addressed in the next chapter.)

5. *You should never consult with others* in lieu *of strategizing for yourself.* Nehemiah did not consult with the few who went with him on the tour of the wall. There is much to be gained from unbiased observation. This does not negate seeking the counsel of others on a subject, but know for yourself as much about the facts as you can. Then, if you do ask others, be sure they have carefully weighed and prayed about their guidance so you are not wrongly influenced. In the end, before you confirm your strategy, pray for the eyes, ears, and mind to understand all that you have learned.

Confession

I have failed miserably to learn this lesson. I am an extrovert, and I would rather process in discussion with others. When I do, it opens the door for the people I am talking to, to weigh in on my plan. Many times these people are shooting from the hip, without careful and clear consideration of the facts. The problem is that once it is said and I have heard it, it requires an action on my part to consider or reject it. Even if I reject it, I may not forget it, and therein lies the problem—I have been influenced. Nehemiah no doubt heard the people talk about the problem they faced, but because they did not know his plan, they couldn't weigh in on his solution. Neither did he invite them to.

Nehemiah is a wise and disciplined leader for us. He was on duty even while visiting with friends and family. Once he found favor with his people and his future employees, he simply did as he had always done before: He perceptively used his eyes and ears to assess the situation. He accessed information from both the people and the landscape so he could confirm his strategy. Then he presented his plan persuasively so he could take the next step: build a team.

3. Team-Build

Then I said to them, "You see the trouble we are in: Jerusalem lies in ruins, and its gates have been burned with fire. Come, let us rebuild the wall of Jerusalem, and we will no longer be in disgrace." I also told them about the gracious hand of my God on me and what the king had said to me.

They replied, "Let us start rebuilding." So they began this good work. (Neh. 2:17–18)

Persuasiveness: the ability to induce or convince by appealing to reason

By this time Nehemiah had assessed the situation in Jerusalem, and he had confirmed his strategy. He was now ready to add people to the plan and build a team. To convince others of a vision, a leader needs *persuasiveness*. A mom does too. Without it, she must resort to authoritarian control, and rules without a relationship lead to rebellion.

Team-Build Persuasively

I think this was a special gift of Nehemiah's. Like my Megan, he was very good at relationships. As you read Nehemiah 2:17–18, watch how he used simple word choices to get immediate buy-in from the people. This is hard for me, and I am always amazed at those people who can easily get others to do what they want. But that's exactly what Nehemiah did. How? Let's take a look at his approach.

- *He was inclusive.* Nehemiah wrote, "Then I said to them . . ." The "them" he was referring to were the Jews, priests, nobles, officials, and others who would be doing the work of rebuilding the wall. It sounds as if Nehemiah called a meeting and included everyone in his plan. This was not the time for secrecy. He wanted everyone to be compelled openly to accept or reject his plan, without any opportunity for someone to hear it incorrectly from another source. When I was young my parents often sheltered us from news we wouldn't like, such as my dad getting transferred to another state. But I could always sense it coming and it made me anxious to wonder. I find it is better to set the truth matter-of-factly before the entire family and invite discussion.

- *He was associative.* Nehemiah was careful to use pronouns such as *we* and *us* to let the people know he had come not to be a ruler over them but to be a leader with them. As a mom this can really help your family team building. When a problem or opportunity arises, present it to all in a family meeting and ask the kids if they have any ideas or solutions. Make it a "together, we can do it" problem solution.

- *He cast a vision.* Though Nehemiah began by reminding the people of *where they were* ("Jerusalem lies in ruins, and its gates have been burned"), he finished by casting a vision of *where they could be* ("Come, let us rebuild the wall of Jerusalem," he said, "and we will no longer be in disgrace"). Some people are really gifted at this. Our high school football coach is one of them. Every year he builds a new group of boys into a highly motivated team by casting a vision. He does it with a different theme every year and for four of the last six years he has led his team to a state championship title. We can do the same as parents if we personally understand and clearly articulate what our families stand for and where we are headed.

- *He was transparent.* Nehemiah told the people without hesitation that it was God's hand and the king's blessing that had made his vision possible. In doing so, he was being transparent. He knew he couldn't do the job alone. Neither can you. You need God, and you need your family's cooperation. And when things are going well in your house, make sure your kids know that the credit is the Lord's.

Team-Build with WOW

Nehemiah had the clout to get the attention of his people. But he needed much more than their attention; he needed a deeply motivated commitment to a project that would involve time, resources, and hard labor. What he did next was to deliver what Michael Hyatt, in his book *Platform*, calls a wow experience. A wow experience is a moment that evokes memorable emotion. For me, a memorable, wow parenting moment came when my youngest, Grant, was ten. It was June, nine months after we had adopted him from Russia. He never went to school in Russia; he was told he was not smart enough. Every day Grant was left in the orphanage with the toddlers. Try to imagine what that did to his intellectual confidence.

My plan his first school year was simply to expose him to children around his age in a very small private school. If he learned to behave in class and to speak English, that was good enough for me. The school was fabulous with agreeing to this plan.

When the school year ended, I assessed and revised the plan. The teacher and I agreed Grant would repeat the grade and that in the coming school year we would begin the academic climb to catch up. But to do that, he needed to be reading by the end of the summer—and I had to teach him. And so the battle began.

We spent the entire summer at the dining room table, Grant refusing and me insisting, over and over and over, to repeat the sounds of the letters of the alphabet. But echoes of negative words about his intelligence were a fierce, daily enemy. Time was running out.

One day I decided it was time to draw a line in the sand. I told him he was not allowed up from the table till he learned that day's lesson. He sat; I sat with him. He refused; I insisted. No meal was offered. Finally, about six thirty in the evening, I told him that he could have dinner *after* the lesson; he ran out the front door in a fit of anger.

He played in the front yard. I called the kids in for dinner. We ate. He didn't. It got dark. He moved to the backyard.

At about ten o'clock, Grant knocked and asked for dinner. I asked if he was ready to do his lesson. He stomped away.

Twelve thirty, I was still up, covertly watching him, which at this point was easy because he was sitting on the back porch. He knocked again, and again I asked if he was ready to do his lesson. This time he said yes. My son learned the sounds of those letters in minutes—then put the sounds together and read the words on that page. He was reading!

I looked at him and smiled. He grinned his wide-faced smile back. It was a wow moment. He *could* learn to read, and I *could* be firm enough to make him. It was a win-win wow for both of us.

Grant had many more learning curves to conquer over the years. But we used that wow lesson as a benchmark. Whenever he was discouraged or obstinately convinced that he couldn't do something, I would remind him that he did learn to read. Whenever I was discouraged and felt I simply could not continue to battle with him, I would remind myself that if I persevered, I could be stronger, and that I had to help him overcome himself. If I didn't, who would?

Wow moments and experiences are inspirational. They provide momentum for persuading us to do more, work harder, reach higher, dream bigger. Michael Hyatt is clear in *Platform* that not every moment can be a wow one, but we need to be able to recognize wow moments when they come and use them to motivate. Nehemiah knew he had a wow opportunity to do something for his people and his God, and he created his wow experience with:

surprise—he arrived with an entourage from the king, without explanation.

anticipation—he visited for three days, without a word about why he was there.

resonance—he touched the people's hearts by inviting them to build with him.

transcendence—his purpose was clearly higher than himself, and he told the people that God's hand was on him.

clarity—he stated the problem simply, and then gave the solution: "Let's build a wall!"

universality—he gave a reason that made *everyone* buy in to his plan: they would no longer be in disgrace.

immediacy—his attitude was not focused on the past and the defeat they suffered, but on "This is now; let's do it."

privilege—he mentioned the king and God as opportunity providers and backers.

As a result of Nehemiah's presentation, the people realized the wow of what God was doing though Nehemiah, and they fell in with the plan.

I think I could have had a lot more wow in my daily parenting, particularly with how I treated homework. There was always so much of it with five kids that I just wanted it to be done every day. I could have added some surprise; I could have made it less an object of dread and more a task of exploration. I could have celebrated wow moments when a child "got" a difficult concept or completed a huge project. I think it is easy to think of creating wow in big projects like Nehemiah's, but can we as moms challenge ourselves to create wow in the daily tasks of our lives? It will take an attitude of wonder and joy for life and knowledge of how God is moving in our families.

Team-Build with Love for Your Unique Team

When the opportunity to adopt older children arose for us, a lot of spectators questioned our decision. In fact, I was surprised at how bold some people were in voicing their concern that we were making a mistake. Children are *never* a mistake. In any case, after being nonplussed the first few times people approached me, I developed my thoughts and this response. I was not afraid of what I would "get" with my adopted children for the same reason I was not afraid of what I would "get" with my biological children. I did not choose any of my children, biological or adopted (though I did have a bit of choice with the adopted: I got to choose between boy or girl—and I chose both!). God does all the choosing, and we need to realize that and be content with our team—love them for who they are. Nehemiah never once complained about his team. He loved them with passion and accepted that it was his responsibility to lead them as they were.

These are your children; love them as they are. Do not pine for somebody else's child, a well-behaved son, or an intelligent daughter. Remember: your days are numbered. The essence of your life with your child is not to achieve but to relate. Your children are your team. Graciously, thankfully, humbly love your team as God loves you, the leader he chose for that very team.

Thoughtfully consider that God chooses his team differently than most spectators would like. His choices don't always make sense. His players aren't always voted "most likely to succeed" or "best" anything. They usually are quite an eclectic group. But he chose them anyway.

Remembering that God chose your children for you is challenging. We can either be frustrated with our team or we can get so wrapped up in our team's drive to achieve that we tend to forget that they belong to God and that he has a plan for them that usurps any plan that we have created without consulting him.

THE PASSIONATE MOM MUST HAVE A PLAN

A passionate mom must protect and ensure a future for her child. She must be a strong wall of bricks and mortar. The future she affords will depend on her goal for her child and how well she maintains her purpose in her plan.

In our story we have focused much on the wall, the inherent function of which is protection or separation. You will want to protect, but it should not become your goal. Protection is simply a means to an end. You will protect as you train your children for their future and independence; that is why there are gates in the wall. You must train and test your children for the day when they will walk through the gates for good to begin a life *outside* the wall, away from you. The end goal, then, is provision: the provision of all the character and skills necessary for a life independent of you—dependent on God. Your child needs to learn how to safely navigate the world outside the gates, and that's what we'll talk about next.

The Brick	The Mortar
Planning	Discernment
	Persuasiveness

Interlude

Opening the Gates

You are so many things to your child. You are a wall—the woman of perception, patience, and prayer who will protect your child. And you are the gatekeeper—the one who will ponder, plan, and persevere in training your child for a future beyond the wall. The wall is the foundation for protecting, and the gates are the opportunity to test your child's readiness to live well outside the wall. Each gate is an opportunity for your child to explore and exercise his or her growing independence by temporarily leaving your protection and venturing out. For you, it affords the opportunity to observe and test your child, to see if he or she is prepared for the freedom the gate has to offer.

THE GATE OF OPPORTUNITY

Sometimes we think of gates as problems in the making. But in reality gates are a good thing. Let me explain.

Have you ever taught a class, or can you remember your classroom days? The teaching process begins with a lesson. When the teacher feels her students have learned one concept, she moves on to another, and then another. After a few lessons, the teacher pauses to gauge the depth of her students' knowledge by giving a quiz. The purpose of the quiz is twofold. First, it will help the teacher better instruct her students. Based on questions the students answer incorrectly, she will know what they did not learn. Second, it will reveal to the students where they have a learning deficit. This will help them better prepare for the *big* test. Without the quiz, neither the teacher nor the students would be aware of knowledge gaps that could result in failing the class. The quiz, therefore, is a good thing. It is an opportunity to test.

The gates in the development of your child's life are also opportunities to test. For instance, let's say your son wants a cell phone. You agree that there would be some safety benefits to being able to contact him readily. So you purchase a phone. But before you allow him to walk through the cell phone gate, you give a lesson: the phone is primarily for safety, you teach him, and it should be used sparingly, no more than 20 minutes a day or 600 minutes a month.

Every month you check the bill to see how much your child is using the phone and if he is making wise choices in whom he is calling. If he is, then your son was ready for the opportunity and you may choose to open the gate wider by allowing texting or a smartphone in the future. If he is not handling the opportunity well, then you can try to reteach the lesson or close the gate for a while by taking the phone away.

FIVE GATE RULES TO REMEMBER

There are lots of gates in life. In this interlude we will cover ten common gates: choices, school, friends, free time, technology, cell phones, social media, driving, dating, and college. Before we evaluate the gates, here are some general rules that apply to all gates:

Gates Must Be Opened and Closed by Parents

> After the wall had been rebuilt and I had set the doors in place, the gatekeepers . . . were appointed. I put in charge of Jerusalem my brother Hanani, along with Hananiah the commander of the citadel, because he was a man of integrity and feared God more than most people do. I said to them, "The gates of Jerusalem are not to be opened until the sun is hot. While the gatekeepers are still on duty, have them shut the doors and bar them. Also appoint residents of Jerusalem as guards, some at their posts and some near their own houses." (Neh. 7:1–3)

It is clear from this account that Nehemiah felt the gates were very important. First, he trusted only two people to oversee them, his brother and Hananiah, a man who feared God. I think a mother must fear God more than anything if she is to be able to say no to a child. Your child may be attracted to the lovely things of the world. But you must fear God more than you fear your child's anger or you may say yes to things that are not in your child's best interest. You must also *love* God and his desires more than you love to please your child.

Honestly, at times this has seemed hard to me. When a child is begging for something, insisting she is ready, and you want to believe her, you feel so mean, but every instinct is saying, *Nope, don't do it*, even though your child is crying. The bottom line is, you really have to *fear* God more than you *love* your child. It's tough. But you are the gatekeeper. You are the one God trusted to monitor the gates.

Gates Are Opened as Privileges, Not Rights

A child should not be entitled to a privilege "just because." A privilege earned will be treated with respect. It may surprise you that I consider gates such as school a privilege. After all, the law requires that children attend school . . . but there are lots of different ways they can do that. One of my children lived her first twelve years in a very small village. When we adopted her, we placed her in a very small school. She is really bright and she excelled there. But when she aged up to a larger middle school, despite her great academic ability, she did poorly. She had become distracted. I reminded her that this new school was a great opportunity but also a great privilege, but in time, the social aspects were too great a temptation, and she lost the privilege of attending that school. We homeschooled after that, all the way through two and a half years of high school—and my smart child finished fast without distractions.

Gates Are Not Opened Based on Age

Some children are ready for an opportunity at one age; others, years later. One of your children may be ready to drive at sixteen, and one may not. If you tell them at an early age that the privilege must be earned, they will not like it, but they will be more likely to try to be ready.

We tend to feel that we must do what the Joneses do. You will hear at some point from your child, "But, Mom, *everybody* my age has one," or, "But, Mom, I am the *only* one my age who is not allowed." And you may be tempted to believe it. Most often, though, if you investigate, you will find that your child's statement is not accurate. There's at least *one* other crazy mom who sees it your way!

Gates Opened Can Always Be Closed

It is easy to get frustrated with kids who are not handling privileges well. If you find you are repeatedly asking them to put the phone away or leave the video game to come to the table, then close the gate for a time. It does get harder to close a gate the longer you wait, so close it sooner rather than later. Once closed, make sure that the child is really ready before you open it again. This is different from taking away a privilege as a consequence. With a consequence the object is usually taken away for a defined time period. When you close a gate, do not feel that you have to give a reopen date. You will find that a child will try harder if he knows he has to prove himself for it.

Gates Must Be Watchfully Guarded

It is clear that Nehemiah never wanted the gates to be left unattended. There would be no opportunity for deeds done in secret. The gates were not opened until the sun was hot. They were shut at night by the gatekeepers and guarded by the residents. Oh, what a world it would be if all moms would band together to watch the gates!

Are you passionate enough to be part of a new generation of mothers who not only guards her own gates but will band together with other moms to help them guard theirs? If we all worked together, I really do believe we could change the world!

THE GOLDEN GATES

The gates that beckon our children to independence are more golden than ever before! In fact, they are downright beautiful and are a temptation to even the most self-controlled adult. Who isn't wowed by the color and magical functionality of the iPhone? What eye cannot appreciate the lifelike experience and surreal engagement of Xbox or Wii? What mind can ignore the wealth of personal information that awaits your fingertips on the ever-evolving platform of social media? I confess: I love technology and the sleek efficiency of what that gate has to offer. Gates are opportunities, but if misused, any gate can be an enticing distraction. And technology is just one of them.

My friend Paige has very young children. When she shared the following story with me, I laughed so hard, and then it hit me: there is so much more moms have to perceive today! Paige and I are not even a generation apart, and yet the things that will tempt her children are already different from what mine faced. But whatever temptations are outside the gate, they must be mastered. This is Paige's story about her precious Finley, age three, who is not quite ready for the gateway to technology, or in this case, the "black present."

The history of this story is that Finley calls the iPad her "black present" because it has a black otter box casing around it to protect it from drops and falls. Two weeks ago, at four thirty in the morning, Finley came running into our room, screaming, "Donald Duck is dead!" My initial response was, this is a dream. Then I forced myself to focus on the clock, and finally, I attempted to try to understand what my baby was babbling about. I had no clue. So like any good, exhausted mother of two children under the age of four, I ushered her into our bed and told her to go to sleep.

Morning dawned and the Donald Duck drama was pushed aside in the scurry to get the day going. Of course, mysteries have a way of presenting clues even when you are not looking. When I was dressing Finley, I noticed her panties were on inside out. Clue #1: she must have gone to the bathroom in the middle of the night. The closest bathroom to her room is the guest bath, so I went to do a little potty check to make sure there weren't any late-night accidents. That's when I saw clue #2: the iPad on the guest bed. I had left it on the kitchen counter the night before. My memory did an instant rewind of the 4:30 a.m. tale of a dead duck, and a new scenario began to unfold in my mind. It was a sweet little scene of Finley rising in the dark to go potty. Fully awake after her successful potty trip, she floated into the kitchen to retrieve the "black present." She then climbed up on the guest bed to watch her beloved Mickey Mouse clubhouse on YouTube until the iPad ran out of juice, or in her words, until "Donald Duck died!"

Needless to say, the black present became a lost privilege that Finley has not yet been given back. The discussion that followed the misdemeanor was a rich opportunity to talk about disobedience and sneaking and trust. Later that afternoon, in the car, I brought it up again and said, "Finley, when you disobey Mommy and Daddy, it makes us so sad. Do you know who else it makes sad?"

Finley answered right away, "God, Mommy!"

"Yes, it makes Jesus so sad when you disobey us. You need to make better choices."

And then my precious, honest little Finley said with a sigh of conviction, "But, Mommy, it makes me sooo happy!"

I tried so hard not to laugh. When I retold the story to my husband, we were both amazed that a three-year-old could verbalize with such clarity the concept of temptation and sin! She had nailed it on the head—it makes us happy, temporarily.

TEN GATES THAT LEAD TO INDEPENDENCE

Nehemiah's wall had several gates, and they were very important because it was through those gates that the Israelites transacted business with the world. Your child also has business to conduct with the world; therefore, it is very important to not isolate her from it until college. It can be better to expose, train, and test her for wisdom as she interacts while she is still under your care. Your wall should also have gates, and at the right time and in the right way, you need to open them. Different children are ready for different kinds of gates at different times.

Caution: Open Carefully!

So just when you think you have the wall in place, your child discovers another gate she is dying to open. Perceive, ponder, and pray before you do. Every child should be individually assessed for "gate" readiness. And no mom should be afraid of closing the gate if the child proves unready. Your child will learn to take privileges seriously if you are unafraid to remove them when abused. There were ten gates in the wall Nehemiah built. Here are the top ten gates I found to be the most important right now, and lessons I learned about how and when to open them.

1. The Choices Gate

Every child must learn to make wise choices on the path to adulthood. Little children make little choices and are rewarded by being given bigger choices. But when little children are given the opportunity to make big choices or lots of choices—or worse, they contest a choice their mothers have already made—difficulties may arise. Here's an example:

> MOM: Honey, we're going to the zoo, so please put your sneakers on.
> CHILD: I don't want to wear my sneakers. I want to wear my sparkle shoes.
> MOM: But we'll be walking a lot, and your tennis shoes are comfy.
> CHILD: So are my sparkle shoes.
> MOM: I don't think they are . . . and we need to go.
> CHILD: But, Mommy!
> MOM: Okay, okay. If you think you will be okay, wear them.

Two things could happen here. On the one hand, the child may end up with blisters and learn a lesson—that would be a good thing. On the other hand, the child may not have blisters, and her desire to challenge her mother's choices has been reinforced. Either way, Mom should never have opened the choice gate and allowed her child to override the decision she had *already* made.

Here's another:

MOM: Honey, would you like to ask Carter to come
over and play?
CHILD: I want to have Ben over.
MOM: But the last couple of times you've played with
Ben, things got out of control. And you got in
trouble together at school.
CHILD: You just don't like Ben.
MOM: Of course I like Ben. I just thought it would be
nice to have Carter over . . . but you can ask Ben, if
you promise to behave.

Same situation. Both of these mothers *knew* what was best for their child. They just didn't assert their wisdom (and their authority). In the first example, the mom felt time pressure. She didn't want to battle in the interest of time. In the second example, the child was a little older, and knowing his mom well, he made her feel guilty by insisting that she didn't like Ben.

When a mom concedes, she is sending a message that may lead her child to believe that Mom doesn't really know what she is doing because she doubts herself and gives in. The child, in comparison, feels so strong that he becomes convinced that he knows what is best for himself.

When children are very young, concessions such as these

can be harmless, but fast-forward ten years. These children have grown up believing that it is *always* their right to choose what's best for themselves—what they wear or whom they play with—and that their mother doesn't really know what is best or she wouldn't back down so easily.

Let's say the girl, now a teenager, comes downstairs to go out, dressed in a skirt twelve inches above her knees and a top made of six inches of fabric. Her father takes one look and tells her to go put some clothes on. Her mom suggests a different top, and the teenager indignantly retorts, "Since when do you tell me what to wear?" She then drives off with a boy that neither parent has ever met, without bothering to say where she is going or what time she will be home.

Guarding the Gateway to Choices

Innocent choices for toddlers can mean trouble for teenagers. Those choices include every who, what, where, and when of their day—for example: who they play with, what they wear or eat, what they watch on TV, what games they play, where they go and with whom, when they wake, play, work, sleep—until they consistently demonstrate to you that they have wisdom to make the choice themselves. Most kids will have areas where they are really wise and make good choices, and other areas where they don't. My daughter, for example, had great discernment in friends very early on. However, she was easily enamored with fashion, and it took time for her to develop the ability to say no to styles that were inappropriate. I was off the hook early as the friend gatekeeper but on duty as the "what not to wear" gatekeeper.

I hope this doesn't sound controlling. In fact, it is quite the opposite. The goal is to slowly open each gate until you no longer have to guard it at all by the time your children graduate high school. They earn the right to choose by demonstrating the ability to choose wisely. Your gatekeeper job should diminish the older they get.

Pray for your child to make wise choices. This prayer is taken from 1 Kings 4:29:

Lord, please give _____ wisdom and very great insight, and a breadth of understanding as measureless as the sand on the seashore.

2. The School Gate

School is an amazing gateway to opportunity. It is also a growing responsibility with each year that passes. There is a lot of freedom in school. There is the opportunity for your child to choose friends and to spend time with them, void of your supervision. Different schools present different temptations for different children. The good news is, there are lots of options today: charter schools, private schools, even virtual schools. I confess I have done them all—public, private, military, Christian, home, and virtual school. Do not be afraid to explore options. Break the mold if your child doesn't fit in it.

Guarding the Gate to School

The best way to guard this gate is to be involved with your child's school. Be the team mom, homeroom mom, backstage mom, or PTA mom! There is a volunteer opportunity for everyone whether you work or not. It does take energy, but the blessing will be that you will be at the gate when you are needed.

God will give you the eyes to see what you need to see. If the freedom a school offers is too much for your child, as it was for one of mine, do not hesitate to explore other options.

Pray for your children while they are at school. The following prayer is based on Hebrews 13:17:

Lord, please give _____ confidence in his leaders at school, and help him to submit to their authority, because they keep watch over him as those who must give an account. Give _____ a desire to do this so that his teachers' work will be a joy, not a burden, for that would be of no benefit to him.

3. The Friendships Gate

Friends can be a sweet blessing. The ability to choose the right friends is a gift for some, learned for others, and an evasive skill for others. Friends are such a necessary, fun part of a child's life that we can think of them as benign. The contrary is true. Paul profoundly stated that thousands of years ago: "Do not be misled," he wrote. "'Bad company corrupts good character'" (1 Cor. 15:33).

Guarding the Gateway to Friendships

People are influenced by those with whom they spend time; therefore, this is a gate that requires careful monitoring. I came across a pamphlet during a time when I was really questioning my parenting ability. My child had decided, with friends, to pursue riskier and more "entertaining" ways to have fun. The pamphlet was entitled *Help for Distressed Parents*, from a lecture offered by Cotton Mather. This is what it said:

Be especially inquisitive what company they (your children) keep. If you leave them to be the companions of fools, they will soon be destroyed fools themselves. Wherefore, do all you can to rescue them from all the snares and haunts of all evil company. Oh, forewarn them and withhold them, as much as you can, from those knots of profane gaming, scoffing, drinking and unclean wretches that keep so many of our young people in the bond of iniquity forever. And the evening after the Sabbath, when, alas there is more villainy, they say, done among us than all the nights of the week besides, if they will then be singularly exposing themselves unto temptation don't you consent unto it, but confine them with our own watchful eye at home upon them.

I shall say no more, but set before you Proverbs 29:15: "A child left to himself bringeth his mother to shame." It seems the mother is usually most ready to let them have their wills; and, lo, she pays for it.

Mr. Mather gave this lecture in Boston on December 14, 1694—more than three hundred years ago. Now, I don't know about you, but I was surprised to hear that teen trouble was a problem in the 1600s. And it seems it was a common problem. Where did "the wretches that keep so many of our young people in the bond of iniquity" come from back in the seventeenth century? There were no pornographic websites, drive-through liquor stores, or online video games. As dramatic as Mather was, I love his gate-related points:

- Be inquisitive about the company your children keep. (Guard the gate!)

- Rescue them from bad company. (Close the gate.)
- Say no when they want to go out on weekends with bad company. (Close the gate.)
- The mom will pay for it if she lets them have their way. (She didn't watch the gate.)

The gateway to friendship is tricky and has been forever. Pray for your child's friendships. Try these simple prayers:

Give _____ friends who love at all times, and brothers born for a time of adversity (based on Proverbs 17:17).

Show _____ how to walk with the wise and become wise, for a companion of fools suffers harm (based on Proverbs 13:20).

4. The Free Time Gate

Free time is a gate that is hard to supervise with a concrete plan. It starts off so innocently because young children play in their free time, and that play is developmental. As children age, they become attracted to things that may not be developmental or wise uses of their free time. Things like television, social media gossip, and video games are all entertaining but not wise uses of free time. And if a child is left to choose, many will choose technology.

We all need downtime, and to relax, some choice is necessary. The trick for a mom is to have structure and guidelines so that a little downtime doesn't become a distraction from worthy pursuits.

Guarding the Gate to Free Time

As your children age up, use perception to observe their natural selections for entertainment. If they always want you to play with them, social interaction with people may be important to them. If they always want to watch TV, then you may want to ponder how you will structure usage parameters for screen time. If they develop crushes at age six, you may want to have conversations about relationships with the opposite sex. It may sound silly at six, but some kids explore "going out" at nine and ten years old, and some parents encourage it. If you don't plan on being in that category, start talking about it early, before your child starts talking about it at school.

Guarding the gate to free time takes perception, pondering, and planning. If your child has a natural bent regarding how they use their free time, use it for good. If they like to play outside with balls, put them on a team. If they like to draw, find an art teacher, or supply them with paints. If you turn off the TV, computer, and other easy forms of entertainment, they will go find something else to do.

Pray for your child to wisely use their free time:

> *Lord, help _____ to understand that you have given him much, and from everyone who has been given much, much will be demanded; and from the one who has been entrusted with much, much more will be asked. Help _____ to appreciate and use the time you have given him wisely (based on Luke 12:48).*

5. The Electronics Gate

This gate leads to today's most popular entertainments: television, computers, music, movies, video games . . . I have covered much of why this is a gateway privilege. Anyone, adult or child, can lose himself in electronics for hours a day.

Electronics are not evil. They are wonderful tools for learning and entertainment, but they do require wisdom and self-control. There are good choices and bad to be made in what you allow your child to watch, listen to, and play. The stakes in the choices are getting higher. Television and movies are more explicit today than even ten years ago. The Internet is bigger and full of pornography. Music can be provocative, abusive, and encourage illegal behavior.

This is a gate that takes constant surveillance. The private and public sectors of our nation have released study after study on the dangers of explicit images and music. We are unwise as a nation in many ways. And as was true for Nehemiah, there are very few people you can trust to guard this gate, including Hollywood and the government. Many people will argue that it's "just" music or a movie, but the studies don't lie: music and movies do make impressions.

Guarding the Gate to Electronics

There are lots of things you can do to protect your child from the dangers of electronics and to prepare him to use self-control when given the privilege:

- *Stay ahead of your child.* Most parents are behind their children when it comes to the latest in technology. Kids today have social network websites, download music both legally and illegally, publish information about themselves that others can see, enter into online dialogue with strangers, and surf the Internet for the latest information, both good and bad. As a parent, you have to learn what's out there and how the system works. In other words, go where your children want to go before they do.

- *Keep all electronics in a public place.* Children should not have electronics in their rooms. The temptations are too great. The computer and television should be in a place where Mom or Dad can walk by and see what's going on.

- *Establish accountability.* Check up on your kids often. Look at the history of the sites they've visited. If they are erasing the history, then you can assume something is wrong; take action accordingly by installing monitoring software. Read the messages they are receiving and sending. You don't have to do this secretly. Your child should already know that accountability is required for Internet use. Use a contract; you can download one at iMOM.com/tools.

- *Install a filter, and password-protect the computer and TV.* Filters provide the safeguard of preventing access to offensive sites. Most filters allow you to choose the degree of filtering based on the age of the child. Password-protect the computer and television so they are only on when you want them to be on, and set channel parameters.

- *Set up family screen-time rules.* The needs, age, development, character, and maturity of each child should be taken into account as you set up guidelines for screen time. This doesn't just involve rules against visiting forbidden sites but also means rules that prohibit wasting time or being consumed by particular games or entertainment. Computer and video game addiction can start very young, so setting firm limits is essential for balance in a child's life. Set up appropriate boundaries for your children and a system for monitoring them. If the child is not being responsible in other areas of family life, is getting poor grades, or is developing some attitude issues, screen time may need to be reduced.

• *Review movie and music choices.* Many parents allow their children to see or listen to whatever they want. This can be a hard gate to monitor. At iMOM we heard about this concern from a lot of moms, so we developed media monitors (www.imom.com/moviemonitor; www.imom.com/musicmonitor) so that parents can teach their children to think about the movies and music they want beforehand. Every movie has a colored graph that charts the level of sex, language, violence, drugs, nudity, and more. It is easy to read and gives a great jumping-off point for discussions of why the movie is or is not appropriate for your child to see. The music monitor is a simple list of the top songs, with a sample of the lyrics. Sometimes, if your kids see the lyrics written in black and white, they will decide on their own not to buy the song! See Resources page 231.

Confession

When my children were young, our cable company was supporting a local man who owned all the strip bars in our city. They had allowed him to have a lower channel for his programming. Our children were passing the channel every day, and my friend walked into her family room one day after school to find her young sons being entertained by pornography. My friend made it a fight with the city council, and we all canceled our cable in protest. She won the battle, but afterward we decided we didn't really miss the cable and left it off.

I had a good chuckle one day when I overheard my kids discussing the possibility that maybe we were the only ones without cable because we were poor! We used the cable money to invest in really good movies, and it didn't really bother my girls. Then my sons began to get older and a love for sports kicked in. We decided that if we wanted to watch games at our house, we had to get cable. We enjoy sports as a family, so it was a great addition; however, it was something I had to monitor with the boys, which I never had to with the girls. It is hard to hold the front on all sides as a mom when you keep adding sides. I confess that I let my standards slip as the boys became teenagers. You have to choose your battles with gates. But there were times when I wished I had not opened the gate to cable at all.

Pray for your child's protection:

Lord, please guard _____'s heart, for everything
he does flows from it. Keep _____'s mouth free
of perversity; keep corrupt talk far from his lips. Let
_____'s eyes look straight ahead; fix his gaze
directly before him. Cause _____ to give careful
thought to the paths for his feet, and help him to
be steadfast in all your ways (based on Proverbs
4:23–26).

6. The Cell Phone Gate

Most cell phones are now smartphones. And most smart-phones are everything a child could want in what could be considered the ultimate toy for all ages. In that tiny, boxy toy are a camera, thousands of games, music, video, Internet, plus the added value of unlimited, unrestricted access to friends via texting, FaceTiming or Skyping, posting, pin-ning, tweeting, Instagraming, and by the time this book is printed, probably some other fascinating form of communi-cation. Kids can hold the world in the palms of their hands. They don't hang out with family anymore. You see them everywhere in restaurants and malls, hanging out with their hands. They never look up; their eyes are fixed on their fin-gers as they glide and punch their beautiful, captivating toy phones.

Guarding the Gate to Cell Phones

More than 75 percent of teenagers have cell phones. That doesn't even include children as young as six who are getting phones. The pace of life demands that families simultaneously run in multiple directions: to work meetings, soccer practice, piano lessons, tutoring sessions, dance class, and more. It's a wonderful convenience to be able to redirect or rearrange transportation on the fly with your kids through the cell phone. Other parents value the safety aspect of giving their children a phone. But you must weigh these pluses against a growing list of cons when trying to decide if you are ready to open this gate. So consider:

- *Is your child ready?* Just because the majority of your child's friends have something doesn't mean that your child should. Has she demonstrated self-control and responsibility? How consistently your child obeys the rules regarding other types of technology to which she already has access (Internet, TV, video games) is a good indicator of how well she will respect and obey the rules you lay down for cell phone use. If you're constantly having to police and correct your child's use of other media, you'll have an even greater battle on your hands with the cell phone, because she'll be using it outside of your sight 99 percent of the time.
- *Are you ready?* You will have to monitor the phone, set parameters, and guard the gate steadfastly. Are you ready for the responsibility?
- *Download a contract.* I love contracts because they ensure clarity. We have lots of them at iMOM. A link to the iMOM Cell Phone Contract can be found in the Resources section (p. 231). Fill it out, and go

over the expectations you have for your child's use of the phone. If he does not meet your expectations, you will have clear recourse explained on the contract, and he will not have an argument for the consequences. See Resources page 231.

- *Start simply.* For safety and family organization, all your child needs is a phone with which he can place and receive voice calls; anything added to that is for entertainment.

- *Use parental controls.* Some phones have parental controls that you can set and password-protect. This is so important if your child has Internet access on his phone. It doesn't help to filter the computer in your house while allowing your son to run around town with unfiltered access to pornography on his phone.

- *Circle the wall often.* This is a privilege you will have to circle often to see for yourself if your child is handling it responsibly. As Nehemiah did, you may have to do it without permission if you suspect there is a need to. That means you should check the phone for inappropriate texts, music, apps, and games.

- *Stand firm.* You must have the backbone to limit its use and take it away if necessary. I have found it difficult to give up my ability to conveniently contact the child if I take her phone away. Only you know if you have the resolve to do what's best for your child—despite the tears and protests—if the phone becomes a problem. If you can't honestly say that you'll pull the plug and set limits, don't buy the phone.

Pray for your child's focus:

> *Teach _____ that time is short, Lord. If he buys*
> *something, help him treat it as if it were not his to*
> *keep. When he uses things of the world, like a cell*
> *phone, help him use it without being engrossed in*
> *it. Remind him that this world in its present form*
> *is passing away and that nothing he owns is of real*
> *importance (based on 1 Corinthians 7:29–31).*

7. The Social Media Gate

Like the gates before it, social media can be addictive and requires a child (*and me*) to have self-control. A child must also be well versed on what is and is not appropriate to post. One other warning: most social media contains elements of either gossip or self-promotion; neither of these adds to a child's character, and time invested in either can be detrimental.

Guarding the Gate to Social Media

- *Defer.* For as long as possible, do not allow participation in social media. You can use me as your mean example. My kids weren't allowed until their senior year of high school. And I relented then only because I wanted them to learn while at home so I could walk them through expectations.
- *Assess your readiness.* Are you ready to monitor? Do you have your child's passwords, and are you committed to checking often? Is your child ready?

- *Start simply.* Train your child about privacy and appropriate uses, and start with all of the settings on the highest level of privacy. To begin, you may want them to allow only family members as friends.
- *"Friend" and follow.* Make sure your child includes you in his online socializing so you can teach him how to use it safely. And have access to all his passwords so you can view his private communication.

Pray for your child to use discretion:

Lord, give _____ the discernment to watch her ways and keep her tongue from sin. Help _____ put a muzzle on her mouth while in the presence of the wicked (based on Psalm 39:1).

8. The Driving Gate

Of all the things a mom needs to do to train her child, this is my least favorite. I would rather potty train ten children than teach one to drive! On so many levels this is a very heavy gate. A car is a weapon. This is a physically dangerous gate for your child and for every innocent person on any road with your child. The irresponsible use of a car can kill someone. The statistics are a reality, and teenagers have more accidents than any other age group. But we consider it a right of age because the law says you can get a license at sixteen.

Cultural advancement has added to a parent's need to perceive the dangers of this gate just as it has in the technology and cell phone gates. Your parents did not need to train you to use self-control on the computer or smartphone. Yet you must train your child. The same is true with driving. There is more traffic in most areas of the country today. There are more gadgets to play with in cars today. And then there is that enticing phone, which most teenagers cannot resist looking at even when they are driving.

Lastly, driving is a giant step forward to independence, especially if your child owns a car. You must be able to trust that he is where he says he is and that commitment to abide by your rules is firm. Toward the end of the sophomore year of high school, most teenagers begin to explore with their free time. It is an age of experimentation, and having wheels greatly enhances their opportunities. It is a time when boundaries need to be clearly established.

Guarding the Gate to Driving

- *Talk about it.* Long before it is time to get a learner's permit, talk about your expectations for the privilege of driving. Ask your child these questions: (1) Can we trust you to do the right thing when we are not around? (2) Are you being responsible in all other areas of your life, such as grades? (3) Is your attitude respectful?
- *Train hard.* Take every opportunity during the permit phase to train for the responsibility. This is your time to be heard. Your child wants that license, so she will listen. Once she has it, you won't be in the car, and your opportunity to be heard is gone.
- *Use a contract.* See Resources page 231. Just like with the cell phone, having a contract that clearly

spells out your commitments and consequences will help. If the child knows ahead of time what will happen if he breaks a commitment, he will think twice. If he breaks the contract, the consequences are clear and arguments about it are avoided. See Resources page 231.

Pray for your child's safety:

Lord, keep _____ from all harm—watch over her life; watch over her coming and going both now and forevermore (based on Psalm 121:7–8).

9. The Dating Gate

Does *dating* today seem to be synonymous with *drama?* Cell phones and social media affect many of the gates; dating is no different. Increased social awareness has hyped everything up to the point where you can become a star based on the drama you create in your relationships. I have conflicting emotions about dating. There are not many children who have the maturity for a serious relationship. And the point of exploring a relationship should be marriage. But children who are dating are not thinking of marriage; they are simply investing in relationships with the intention of ending them. The result can be self-inflicted heartbreak, drama, and distraction.

Guarding the Gate to Dating

- *Talk about it early.* Decide if your family is going to allow dating; at what maturity level (not age, because not all children are ready at the same time); and what parameters you will have.

- *Defer it.* It will never hurt to make a child wait to date. When my children first began to chat about someone "going out" with someone in middle school, I interjected immediately that we do not "go out" when we can't really *"go* out" yet. In other words, they were not allowed to declare a relationship without permission, and they knew that I thought it was strange that kids who can't even "go out" without a parent taking them somewhere said they were "going out."

- *Interview candidates.* Set parameters for the exploration of a relationship. One rule should be that you are required to meet the child—boy or girl. My husband interviewed the boys who dated our girls. The knowledge of the required interview got around, and my girls insist that is why they didn't get to date much because the boys thought twice about it. I think that alone weeded out some unnecessary dating.

- *Discuss physical intimacy.* Self-control for anyone, let alone a teenager, is difficult in the midst of passion. Joe White is the owner of Kanakuk Kamps. He has an amazing way of communicating with teens that resonates with them. My kids attended his camps, and I was always amazed that they could remember his lessons with clarity. I asked Joe if I could share what he shares with the kids about self-control in physical intimacy. This is it, complete with discussion questions:

How Far Is Too Far?

"With her many persuasions she entices him; with her flattering lips she seduces him. Suddenly he follows her, as an ox goes to the slaughter, or as one in fetters to the discipline of a fool, until an arrow pierces through his liver; as a bird hastens to the snare, so he does not know that it will cost him his life" (Prov. 7:21–23 NASB).

Three unemployed truck drivers eagerly read the classified ad—"WANTED skilled truck driver to drive a truck filled with TNT through narrow mountain roads." The president of the trucking company interviewed all three men. To each, the same question was asked. "When driving a load of TNT, how close can you get to the edge of the road without falling off the cliff?"

The first man boasted of his great skills. "I can get the rear wheels of the truck 12" from the edge. Never fell off yet." The second driver was even more skilled. "I can get one wheel half-way over the edge and not veer off the pavement." The third driver humbly replied, "TNT is a dangerous load. I'd stay as far from the edge as I can."

Guess who got the job.

Kissing, heavy French kissing, petting over the clothes, petting under the clothes, laying together, sexual intercourse. An automatic transmission shifts gears between one step of sex to the next. That's how God built men and women for pleasure and procreation in marriage.

The first and second truck driver's pride described many kids who get hurt in a variety of ways sexually. The third truck driver describes those who walk the wedding aisle and stay faithfully married with no regrets.

Jesus' death makes you pure. Jesus' love helps you stay that way.

1. *How do you feel about "the edge of the cliff" and how close will you go to the edge?*
2. *Why is sex like a truck loaded with TNT?*
3. *What did you learn today and how will you apply it to your life with the opposite sex?*

- *Get to know the date.* If your child is developing a relationship with someone else, and you have allowed it, you should be developing a relationship with that person too. Then you can observe whether the relationship is having a positive or negative effect on your child. This is your child, and anyone he or she associates with should be of interest to you. Incorporate your child's date into family activities so that everyone can get to know him or her. Some of the most unbiased observations about my children's "special friends," as my husband calls them, have been made by their siblings. Let the family weigh in.
- *Create responsibility and accountability.* There are long-term consequences to physical intimacy that can affect not just your child's life but the lives of others. Relationships require self-control. People are to be esteemed and honored. If your child is not ready to show honor to others with self-control and selflessness, then she is not ready to invest in a relationship.

Pray for your child's relationships:

*May the God who gives endurance and
encouragement give _____ the same attitude
of mind toward each other that Christ Jesus
had, so that with one mind and one voice he
may glorify the God and Father of our Lord
Jesus Christ (based on Romans 15:5–6).*

10. The College Gate

College is a gateway to the American dream and some-times an American idol. So much focus, pressure, and work are put into attaining acceptance to the college of your child's choice, or maybe your choice. Other areas of development, such as character building or spiritual growth, can be sacri-ficed to the academic dream. Much thought is given to getting there, but not much thought about what will be done there. So many kids change majors or graduate with a major that they don't know what to do with. Recently, I saw several creative and entertaining YouTube videos produced by nineteen-year-old boys from Britain as a part of their gap year project. In some countries a gap year is encouraged, usually taken before attending college. The purposes may include independent learning, problem-solving practice, career exploration, and training in internationalism. I think it is brilliant.

In the United States the majority of people would probably think there was something wrong with you if you didn't go to college right away, but not everyone feels that way. I know one young man who did not demonstrate a lot of responsibility in high school. His parents felt he was not ready to take college seriously, so he went into the military. After four years of service, he came back a different person and is taking full advantage of his college opportunity.

Guarding the Gate to College

This final gate, which leads to college, is like the ones before it—a privilege, not a right. When one is given a privilege, he should value it and treat it as treasure. College today costs a treasure! Children will value the opportunity more if you explain it to them early.

College is such a wonderful opportunity for huge steps of adventure, independence, and self-discovery. But it is also an opportunity for temptation. Everything you have taught your children up to this point will be challenged in college. Remember: by this age you have been slowly releasing your control as they have built responsibility and earned trust. They should know your expectations by now. They are adults, and the opportunity is theirs. We told our children that as long as we were paying for their support in college, we expected them to do their best academically and to honor God with their choices. That was all. It was very freeing and so sweet to see them take off!

Pray for your child's future:

Lord, you are the everlasting God, the Creator of
the ends of the earth. You will not grow tired or
weary, and your understanding no one can fathom.
You give strength to the weary and increase the power
of the weak. Even youths grow tired and weary, and

young men stumble and fall; but those who hope in the Lord will renew their strength. They will soar on wings like eagles; they will run and not grow weary, they will walk and not be faint. Give _____ *strength to soar (based on Isaiah 40:28–31).*

THE PASSIONATE MOM MUST BE A GATEKEEPER

You are Nehemiah to your child. You are the mom who will build the walls to protect your child and open the gates to test her. You are the Passionate Mom whose job it is to train your child to wisely take advantage of everything life has to offer. Only you can decide when to open one of the gates in the wall and expose your child to what lies on the other side. Only you will perceive, ponder, and pray with a mother's heart as your child experiences different aspects of the culture through the gate you have opened. You must guide your child in wisdom as he learns to navigate the culture on his own.

We have a wall, and we have gates, and they are almost complete. With just two more bricks, we will be ready for years of parenting. Nehemiah, just like every mother in the world, had problems. We can learn from our fearless leader how to handle our problems with courage as we look at brick #9.

Problem Solving

> The goal of leadership is not to eradicate
> uncertainty but rather to navigate it.
>
> —Andy Stanley*

Life comes with problems, and so do children. There will always be struggles and opposition to your efforts, days and even weeks when you just can't seem to get ahead of the onslaught. Little children have little problems, and bigger children can have bigger problems. All five of my children are within six years of one another—I know it's crazy, but I never planned to adopt two children the same ages as two of my biological children. Then they grew, and I had five teenagers all at one time. It was and still is a fast, furious, and fun roller coaster that we ride a dozen times a day. Every ride is a lot of anticipation on the way up, fear and adrenaline on the way down, and emotional exhaustion

---

* http://www.sebc.edu/wp-content/uploads/2012/08/Lesson-in-Leadership-Journal_
  excerpt.pdf.

when it is over. But given the choice of a life with or without the roller coaster, I would choose to ride, without a doubt. It is my only excuse to be a little disheveled and wind-whipped!

Nehemiah didn't sail through his plan without difficulty, and neither shall we. Nehemiah knew how to navigate through problems. He hadn't even left the palace for Jerusalem when we learn that the opposition began. It happens all the time. You are busy executing the plan and performing with excellence, and out of nowhere, a two-by-four slams you in the face. Nehemiah dealt with four different problems head-on, and with great flexibility altered his plan to overcome them. He battled and he didn't give in, because he had to save his people from disgrace. We must battle too. The buck stops with us, and if we don't fight opposition, who will? This brick is a little different; it reminds us to be on guard and to expect that we will have problems. It is the brick that should have a flashing caution light on it—a reminder that problems will come, but we will not be overcome, because we are ready at all times to take them in stride and keep going.

Brick #9
Problem solving
A Passionate Mom has trials, tribulations, difficulties, and inconveniences—often daily—but she solves them as best she can.

SIX KINDS OF PROBLEMS MOMS MUST FACE

There will always be opposition to your parenting in the form of problems that arise and try to break down the walls or storm the gates. Here are six types of problems that Nehemiah faced, some examples of how they can surface in the mom world, and some possible solutions for these problems.

Problem #1: Jealousy

> When Sanballat the Horonite and Tobiah the Ammonite official heard about [Nehemiah's plan to rebuilt the walls of Jerusalem], they were very much disturbed that someone had come to promote the welfare of the Israelites (Neh. 2:10).

Uh-oh. Here comes trouble. The enemy has taken notice. The Bible says that instead of feeling joy and goodwill, Sanballat and Tobiah were "disturbed" about Nehemiah's intentions. Could they have been jealous because Nehemiah was improving the welfare of the Israelites? Probably so. And similarly, a Passionate Mom has a focus on her family that will make others jealous.

In spite of these men's jealousy, Nehemiah remained confident in his purpose, and if you are a Passionate Mom, you will be confident about your parenting. This does not mean you have it all together, but some other moms will not see that. They will only see that you have confidence in your parenting and that you are enjoying it. A few will become jealous. They may also envy you if your child experiences success of any kind. If your son is a good swimmer, some other mothers will see you and him as competition. If your daughter is smart, there will be moms who view her as competition for honors. If your son or daughter is popular, both parents and other children may become jealous of your child's friendships. So how do you deal with jealousy when you sense it emanating from other parents? You'll find that the solution is the same for this problem as for the next one.

Problem #2: Ridicule

> But when Sanballat the Horonite, Tobiah the Ammonite official and Geshem the Arab heard about it, they mocked and ridiculed us. "What is this you are doing?" they asked. "Are you rebelling against the king?" (Neh. 2:19)

> When Sanballat heard that we were rebuilding the wall, he became angry and was greatly incensed. He ridiculed the Jews, and in the presence of his associates and the army of Samaria, he said, "What are those feeble Jews doing? Will they restore their wall? Will they offer sacrifices? Will they finish in a day? Can they bring the stones back to life from those heaps of rubble—burned as they are?"
>
> Tobiah the Ammonite, who was at his side, said, "What they are building—even a fox climbing up on it would break down their wall of stones!" (Neh. 4:1–3)

Jealousy can incite others to say things that are not true in an attempt to defend why their kids are not in the same favorable situation that yours are. They will put down your efforts and ridicule them, saying things such as:

- "Well, she has time to do all that for her children because she doesn't have to work."

- "She can afford to pay for all those lessons for her children because she works."
- "Well, she can cater to her child's talent because she only *has* one child."
- "Her son only gets A's on all the tests because his sister had that teacher last year."
- "He only made the team because his father has connections."
- "Just because she doesn't allow it doesn't mean her kids won't do it without her permission."

The Solution to Jealousy and Ridicule: Rise Above Them, and Pray

> I answered them by saying, "The God of heaven will give us success. We his servants will start rebuilding, but as for you, you have no share in Jerusalem or any claim or historic right to it." (Neh. 2:20)

Part of your plan to be a better mom is to understand that opposition has a plan too: to discourage you and make you feel that you can't succeed. Nehemiah didn't fall for it; he rose above it, and so can you. And the best, fastest way to rise above anything that is pulling you down is to look up, to the One who rose above it all, including jealousy and ridicule—and pray to him! So Nehemiah prayed—and look at how it turned out for him:

> Hear us, our God, for we are despised. Turn their insults back on their own heads. Give them over as plunder in a

land of captivity. Do not cover up their guilt or blot out their sins from your sight, for they have thrown insults in the face of the builders.

So we rebuilt the wall till all of it reached half its height, for the people worked with all their heart. (Neh. 4:4–6)

Don't you love that last sentence? The jealousy and ridicule seemed only to have motivated the Israelites more, and they worked wholeheartedly. I think they were so inspired by the fearless, clear-sighted, practical newcomer named Nehemiah that they began to believe what he believed. Nehemiah's faith became contagious even in the face **Faith:** trust in God of opposition. And your faith will inspire your children to have faith in the face of jealousy and ridicule. Faith is the character quality that will secure every brick in the wall.

The next two problems are interconnected, and the solution is the same for both. Let's look at each:

Problem #3: Anger

But when Sanballat, Tobiah, the Arabs, the Ammonites and the people of Ashdod heard that the repairs to Jerusalem's walls had gone ahead and that the gaps were being closed, they were very angry. They all plotted together to come and fight against Jerusalem and stir up trouble against it. (Neh. 4:7–8)

Nehemiah's enemies quickly morphed from being green with envy to red with fury. The game had escalated because the Israelites were succeeding in their endeavors, and the wall was half-built.

Anger is cruel. I know from experience. One of my adopted children battles a past filled with neglect and abuse, and anger sometimes overcomes him. When he is consumed and looks at me with confusion, my heart fills with fear for this thorn in his flesh that threatens to harm him.

Similarly, when Nehemiah's enemies became incensed and threatening, the Israelites were filled with fear . . . which is another problem that every mom will face:

Problem #4: Fear

> Meanwhile, the people in Judah said, "The strength of the laborers is giving out, and there is so much rubble that we cannot rebuild the wall."
>
> Also our enemies said, "Before they know it or see us, we will be right there among them and will kill them and put an end to the work."
>
> Then the Jews who lived near them came and told us ten times over, "Wherever you turn, they will attack us." (Neh. 4:10–12)

Now the people were afraid and looking at Nehemiah with questions in their eyes. Have you ever seen fear in the eyes of your child? I have. One of my children battles Addison's disease. Weariness overcomes her, and when she bottoms out and looks at me with sadness, my heart fills with fear for this thorn in her flesh that will threaten her long after I am gone and can no longer help her.

Anger, Fear, and Threats

Anger and fear both involve threat. An angry person may threaten; the fearful one feels threatened. My sister once felt threatened by a neighbor. I have a friend who felt threatened by a teacher because of her faith. Another friend feels threatened by her husband's addiction. Children threaten other children, and every day I read about kids being threatened by bullies.

The Passionate Mom will face anger and threats, and her children will look to her with fear in their eyes. She will also face fears of her own. What can she do?

The Solution: Pray and Be Prepared

> But we prayed to our God and posted a guard day and night to meet this threat. (Neh. 4:9)

When angry enemies threatened Nehemiah and the Israelites, and fear began to set in, what happened? He prayed and they prayed. Can *you* pray? If you haven't yet begun to pray, go back to chapter 4 and work it! We can change this generation of children—if we pray. There are a lot of times when that is *all we can do*. Prayer was a huge part of Nehemiah's plan—in fact, it was the first part, and it should be our first call to action too.

After prayer, courageously prepare.

> Therefore I stationed some of the people behind the lowest points of the wall at the exposed places, posting them by families, with their swords, spears and bows. After I looked things over, I stood up and said to the nobles, the officials and the rest of the people, "Don't be afraid of them.

Remember the Lord, who is great and awesome, and fight for your families, your sons and your daughters, your wives and your homes."

When our enemies heard that we were aware of their plot and that God had frustrated it, we all returned to the wall, each to our own work.

From that day on, half of my men did the work, while the other half were equipped with spears, shields, bows and armor. The officers posted themselves behind all the people of Judah who were building the wall. Those who carried materials did their work with one hand and held a weapon in the other, and each of the builders wore his sword at his side as he worked. But the man who sounded the trumpet stayed with me.

Then I said to the nobles, the officials and the rest of the people, "The work is extensive and spread out, and we are widely separated from each other along the wall. Wherever you hear the sound of the trumpet, join us there. Our God will fight for us!"

So we continued the work with half the men holding spears, from the first light of dawn till the stars came out. At that time I also said to the people, "Have every man and his helper stay inside Jerusalem at night, so they can serve us as guards by night and as workers by day." Neither I nor my brothers nor my men nor the guards with me took off our clothes; each had his weapon, even when he went for water. (Neh. 4:13–23)

When I read Nehemiah's words—"Don't be afraid! Remember the Lord! And fight for your families!"—I feel as if I have been transported into a scene from *Braveheart*, only Nehemiah has replaced William Wallace. Nehemiah was courageous; his confidence was firmly rooted in God. Moms can be just as courageous in the face of anger, fear, and threats to our children. We can also fight—if we are smart and we prepare. Nehemiah fearlessly prepared his people in ways that we can imitate as we lead our children.

First, after he had prayed to his Father (Neh. 4:4, 9), he began to build his people's confidence, reminding his people that there was nothing to be afraid of if they would "remember the Lord" (v. 14). Then he engaged in some highly organized "emergency preparedness." Every person knew just what to do should a problem arise. Organization can bring confidence to your family, and if you will prepare your family as Nehemiah prepared his workers, then whatever may come, you and your children will be as ready as you can be.

Courage: bravery; the moral strength to advance, persist, or endure in the face of fear or trouble

When you have prayed and prepared, you can lead with courage and confidence. And when your children see you leading with courage, they will gain confidence from you. It takes a lot of courage to dare to parent in today's world. Put it in the mortar and mix it in well!

Problem #5: Internal Squabbles

> Now the men and their wives raised a great outcry against their fellow Jews. Some were saying, "We and our sons and daughters are numerous; in order for us to eat and stay alive, we must get grain."

Others were saying, "We are mortgaging our fields, our vineyards and our homes to get grain during the famine."

Still others were saying, "We have had to borrow money to pay the king's tax on our fields and vineyards. Although we are of the same flesh and blood as our fellow Jews and though our children are as good as theirs, yet we have to subject our sons and daughters to slavery. Some of our daughters have already been enslaved, but we are powerless, because our fields and our vineyards belong to others." (Neh. 5:1–5)

Just when you think you have it all under control, opposition can come from within too. Nehemiah's people were tired. They were physically exhausted from building the wall and standing watch. They were emotionally exhausted from the threat of war lurking maliciously beyond the wall. So they got a little cranky when the food got scarce. Have you been in a similar situation? I have. I am there now! As I mentioned earlier, my house flooded three days after I signed the contract for this book. My stuff is either in storage or it has been destroyed. And that goes for my five teenagers' stuff too—that makes them cranky for sure. We are living in half the space with a fraction of our stuff. Now I am building a house, writing a book, working for iMOM, and keeping the family in motion all at once. *I* am cranky!

If outward attacks cannot stop you from being the wall for your child, then internal opposition will try. Internal opposition has been the failing of many a family. "Irreconcilable differences" is the stamp of finality on many a divorce document. Bickering, selfishness, and anger can melt the bonds of family unity. Nehemiah wouldn't allow it, and neither should we.

The Solution: Unselfishness

When I heard their outcry and these charges, I was very angry. I pondered them in my mind and then accused the nobles and officials. I told them, "You are charging your own people interest!" So I called together a large meeting to deal with them and said: "As far as possible, we have bought back our fellow Jews who were sold to the Gentiles. Now you are selling your own people, only for them to be sold back to us!" They kept quiet, because they could find nothing to say.

So I continued, "What you are doing is not right. Shouldn't you walk in the fear of our God to avoid the reproach of our Gentile enemies? I and my brothers and my men are also lending the people money and grain. But let us stop charging interest! Give back to them immediately their fields, vineyards, olive groves and houses, and also the interest you are charging them—one percent of the money, grain, new wine and olive oil."

"We will give it back," they said. "And we will not demand anything more from them. We will do as you say."

Then I summoned the priests and made the nobles and officials take an oath to do what they had promised. I also shook out the folds of my robe and said, "In this way may God shake out of their house and possessions anyone who does not keep this promise. So may such a person be shaken out and emptied!"

At this the whole assembly said, "Amen," and praised the LORD. And the people did as they had promised. (Neh. 5:6–13)

Nehemiah was busy cleaning up from a day of wall building and heard his "children" arguing about food, or lack of it, or the price of it, or the cost of borrowing money to buy it. The selfishness and squabbling disgusted him, and like any good mom, he got angry. Then he . . . *did not* yell. No, Nehemiah pondered (v. 7). So wise, our Nehemiah. He pondered before he spoke, lest he vent a volcano of words that may not have been motivating or edifying. When he finally did speak he addressed the situation with directness in the presence of all. They were being selfish. He then told them exactly what to do to treat each other fairly: Give. Take one for the team. They agreed, and that was the end of that.

If we could do a survey of all the reasons family members have argued, I bet we would discover that the vast majority are rooted in selfishness. The immediate acquiescence that Nehemiah received from his people would probably not be my children's response. My kids would most likely not look at me and so readily agree. We are a strong-willed lot. All the more reason why I cannot let squabbles go, because they will build in intensity and tear apart relationships if left unaddressed.

Marital squabbles are the worst, I think, because the kids witness their parents' bad example. My husband and I have lots of examples of squabbles. I may think our daughter is mature enough to go to homecoming; my husband doesn't. He thinks our son is old enough to hunt; I don't. Next he thinks our son is being disrespectful; I think he is just tired and frustrated from a bad game. You get the picture. We tend to argue most about the kids.

Money is the other big reason couples argue, but there are many more, and in every case, the longer squabbles go unresolved, the bigger they get. And bigger squabbles, if not dealt with, can lead to deeper damage and sometimes even to divorce.

Someone once told me that the average age of the oldest child in most divorces is thirteen. This is precisely when a child most needs a father in the home because developmentally, the child is beginning to exercise the art of debate. I don't know about yours, but my husband can cut through debate with a laser precision that I can't. I tend to get too emotionally involved and can be dragged into aspects that muddle the issue. He doesn't. That's why it's important to resolve marital squabbles early on. Unresolved, they can lead to a break in the leadership team—a team that was meant to work together for the benefit of the child.

Generosity: readiness to give to others

Passionate Moms must passionately fight against internal squabbles. Encouraging unselfishness by calling out self-centeredness and modeling generosity is the first step toward harmony in your family.

─────── **Confession** ───────

The strong-willed Merrill family has a really hard time with generosity. And I confess I have not always addressed selfishness. When we hit the teenage years, it became a lot more work than if I had been on my game when they were younger and more moldable.

Problem #6: Distraction

We are on a very personal mission: to be the best moms we can be so we can protect our children and prepare them for a future. We are our children's leaders, but we can be easily distracted from that mission by sneaky opposition—like the kind we see in Nehemiah's story.

The enemy got mad, bullied, made threats against the "children"—but nothing derailed Nehemiah. Now they were desperate. Sanballat, Tobiah, and Geshem realized that if they wanted to stop the train, they would need to get to the engineer. It was personal; they had to stop one man. But he was a very smart man, so they needed to be sneaky. If they couldn't scare him, then they would distract him from his work.

> When word came to Sanballat, Tobiah, Geshem the Arab and the rest of our enemies that I had rebuilt the wall and not a gap was left in it—though up to that time I had not set the doors in the gates—Sanballat and Geshem sent me this message: "Come, let us meet together in one of the villages on the plain of Ono."
>
> But they were scheming to harm me; so I sent messengers to them with this reply: "I am carrying on a great project and cannot go down. Why should the work stop while I leave it and go down to you?" Four times they sent me the same message, and each time I gave them the same answer. (Neh. 6:1–4)

All but the gates were in place, and that cupbearer had whipped a nation into order! I can just imagine his enemies' frustration: *How did we let this lowly group get this far?* they must have wondered. *How can we get our hands on this guy?*

So they sent an invitation . . . *four* times. And every time, using his well-developed common sense, Nehemiah said no, he could not take his eyes off his work.

What invitations should you be saying no to? A promotion at work that will require travel that takes you away from the "great project" of parenting? Another big sale at the mall that will take time and money that is needed elsewhere? Bunko, bridge, book club? A volunteer position? A higher tennis bracket? The television, computer, or phone? What whispers, *"Come . . ."*? Do you know how to say no?

I have not always been so adept in recognizing attacks as Nehemiah was. Often it is only in hindsight that I realize all that was coming at me from different directions. Had I recognized it, I would have handled it better. This book is the perfect example. These final four chapters have been killer. Every day, hours have been stolen by necessary distractions, like the rebuilding of the house, my husband's book release, a graduation, two moves (one child to Birmingham; another, back home from school), the end of the school year, preparations for summer camp, and of course, a million deadlines at work. And on top of that, Madison, my beloved iMOM wrangler and my right hand, became a first-time mother. Two killer months of distractions! I don't feel as if I handled them with the clarity and strategic concentration that Nehemiah did. I let my emotions play into every task, making me feel overwhelmed and unqualified. I am my own worst enemy; I didn't need a Sanballat, Tobiah, or Geshem. I can fill all three roles against myself: I have been distracted by hours of searching for certain things for the house at a price I can afford when I should have just settled for something less than my idea of perfect. Then, when I realize how much time I've lost, my hours of distraction morph into shame and stress, which I have allowed to threaten my health. I have experienced irregular heartbeats and faintness—not good for a girl with a heart condition.

I am writing this book for me!

The Solution to Distractions

Refuse to give in. Nehemiah refused to give in to distraction; he repeatedly said no to time away from his important work. He was determined. With determination mixed into our mortar, we can fix the problem-solving brick firmly in the wall.

Determination: fixed purpose

THE PASSIONATE MOM MUST SOLVE PROBLEMS

Three whole chapters in the book of Nehemiah detail the problems he encountered and how he adeptly overcame each one. Every life has problems, and every mom must deal with them. You are a leader for your children. How you handle problems will affect them. If you refuse to give in to them, then your children will gain confidence by watching you. Then they will grow up to imitate you. Like Nehemiah's people, they will learn that you are not afraid, that you are committed to parenting them, and that you believe that God will help you accomplish his purpose for you—to be the best mom you can be in raising his children.

And that is the purpose we have pursued to the end of this story—to be the best mom you can be. To do that, there is just one more thing to do . . .

Persevere to the end.

The Brick	The Mortar
Problem Solving	Faith
	Courage
	Generosity
	Determination

10

Perseverance

Five days after I had my first child, Megan, I hemorrhaged and lost so much blood I had to be readmitted to the hospital for several days for surgery and a blood transfusion. Because of those complications, coupled with my heart condition, a second birth would be dangerous, so before we could have another child, we had to weigh the risks. When we felt it was time to have another baby, we intentionally made the choice, despite the risks, to have Emily. Eventually we chose to have a third child, Mark Jr., and again I hemorrhaged. The doctor then advised us that we should be thankful for our three healthy children and should avoid future pregnancies.

Ten years went by, and there was no growth in our family number—until we decided to adopt two children. It was an intentional decision to expand our family.

INTENTIONALITY

I once heard author John Maxwell speak about what he calls the law of intentionality. He said that you will not personally grow automatically. If you want to grow, develop, and change, you must be intentional about it. You must work at it every day. There is only one thing in life that is guaranteed to happen without you working at it, and that is death. Death is automatic. That was an easy point for me to get. My faulty heart has taught me well that the when, where, and how of death will not be my choice; and it will be irreversible. Every day between now and that day, I must be intentional. If I want to grow, I have to choose to do so. If I want my family to grow, I have to make that choice too. If I want to grow in my parenting, I have to intentionally build the wall and monitor the gates.

Maxwell also said that the choice you make, makes you. I can't go so far as to say that the wall you make will make your family, but I do believe it will make a difference in your family because there will be a difference in you. As the mother, so much of what you do affects your children. Every decision we made to have another child was very intentional. I must be just as intentional about how to parent each of those children. Every choice, every day, is either growing you forward or pushing you backward. Moving forward takes intentionality. Intentionality takes perseverance. Perseverance is our final brick, and with it we will accomplish great things for our families.

Brick #10
Perseverance
A Passionate Mom must intentionally
maintain a purpose in spite of problems,
continuing steadfastly until the end.

Nehemiah was intentional about everything he did, from perception to persevering.

PERSEVERING IN PARENTING

As I write this final chapter, there is a tropical storm brewing. I am sitting at a huge window four stories up, facing the churning, wind-whipped Tampa Bay that has flooded three days in a row at high tide. What is it with storms and me? I do love them. Storms can be captivating. For the last three days, Instagram has been full of pictures of the boulevard that runs along the bay totally under water. There was even a creatively edited picture of a shark swimming down the street! Lots of people are venturing out to take unique pictures of the landscape gone wild, even as others are barricading themselves in their homes to avoid having an accident and monitoring the devastation on the news.

There are two sides to every storm—they can be fascinating and they can be frightening. The same could be said of parenting. It can be so fascinating, filled with thrilling adventure and sweet surprises. It can also be so frightening, plagued by agonizing hours and painful unknowns.

Is your family in choppy waters? Or are you in a full-blown hurricane? Did you see it coming, or was it a tornado that just crept out of nowhere? Is it fascinating to you, or frightening?

Have you ever seen the movie *Parenthood*? Gil (Steve Martin) and Karen (Mary Steenburgen) are a married couple with three children. Gil really wants to be a better dad. But persevering through challenges at work and his children's developing emotional issues starts to get to him. Then he finds out that Karen is pregnant with a fourth child. He descends quickly and comically through fear, worry, anxiety, and into panic. Karen, on the other hand, is delighted with the pregnancy and fascinated with each of her children's unique emotional problems.

Right before my favorite scene, Gil tells Karen about the anxiety he experienced watching his son play baseball and his fear that his son would "miss the ball." Karen gets frustrated and says, "What do you want? Guarantees? These are kids, not appliances. Life is messy."

Gil's little grandmother (Helen Shaw) walks in on the conversation and starts rambling. "You know when I was nineteen Grandpa took me on a roller coaster. Up, down, up, down. Oh, what a ride . . . I always wanted to go again. It was just interesting to me that a ride could make me so frightened . . . so scared, so sick, so excited . . . and so thrilled all together. Some didn't like it. They went on the merry-go-round. That just goes around. Nothing. I like the roller coaster. You get more out of it."*

Of course, the meaning of that monologue went right over Gil's head, but not Karen's. Karen knew that Grandma was talking about the ride of her life—parenting her children.

The next scene is my favorite. You can watch it on YouTube at http://www.youtube.com/watch?v=7_WLSh7GE9I. It is The

---

* http://www.script-o-rama.com/movie_scripts/p/parenthood-script-transcript-steve-martin.html.

Parenthood Rollercoaster scene. The family is sitting in a crowded school auditorium for one of their children's school plays. Gil is sulking from the previous roller coaster conversation, and Karen is smiling as she videotapes their daughter on stage. Suddenly, their youngest child jumps out of his seat and runs up onto the stage because the actors, in his mind, are hurting his sister. He creates mayhem, running around on the stage and hitting the other children. Half of the audience are laughing, and the other half are getting angry because the child is ruining the show. Then the room begins to shift, and you hear the crank of a roller coaster pulling up an incline. The set onstage is falling apart, and Karen and Gil are in the middle of the auditorium as the room sways and moves up and down, up and down. Gil and Karen are on the roller coaster of life with children. Karen is thoroughly enjoying every minute of the ride. Gil is hiding his eyes and miserably bracing himself as if he is going to be sick.

Then Gil looks up and sees his daughter with his runaway toddler onstage. They are laughing and playing together in the chaos. He looks at his wife next to him; she, too, is laughing with joy in her eyes. And Gil has a wow moment. This is messy. This is parenthood—unpredictable, frightening, fascinating. You can go with the ride and accept the ups and downs with joy, or you can fight against the ride and descend into fear and anxiety. In that moment Gil makes a choice. He intentionally chooses to enjoy the ride—to persevere through parenting with joy—and it changes his life as a dad.

Nehemiah was never a parent, that we know, but he faced fascinating and frightening situations leading his people, and he chose to ride the roller coaster with excitement and to face the storm with joy. Nehemiah intentionally chose to focus with fascination and wonder on what God might do in the lives of his people if they could persevere and surround their city with protection. With Nehemiah's leadership and God's favor, they finished the wall, and a wonder it became to all who beheld it.

> So the wall was completed on the twenty-fifth of Elul, in fifty-two days.
> When all our enemies heard about this, all the surrounding nations were afraid and lost their self-confidence, because they realized that this work had been done with the help of our God. (Neh. 6:15–16)

CHOOSE LIFE

Nehemiah's mission to protect and provide his people with a future was a calling of the highest order because it was important to the life of his people—just as parenting is important to the life of your child. He chose to value his "children's" lives over his career in the palace, over his personal comfort, even over his own life. Of all the things you do in life, in the end, loving God and investing in the lives you love will be the only things that matter.

God is asking you, in this moment, "What is it you want?" Do you want to protect and provide your children with a future? Do you want to pour perception and pondering and passion and prayer and patience and preparation into a plan so that you can confidently answer yes to the question "Am I doing this right?" Do you want to persevere to the end so you can look back and say, "I was the best mom that I could be"?

Do you even believe that your parenting can make that much of a difference in your child's life?

Nehemiah believed he could be used by God to make a difference in the lives of his people, and he did. Would the wall have been built without him? I believe God would have used someone else to build the wall if Nehemiah had been unwilling. But what about your child? Who will be the wall for him if you are not? Will God have to use someone else, like a coach or teacher, to protect and train your child because you were unwilling?

When I went to Siberia to complete the adoption of two of our children, I met their biological mother. It was heartbreaking. She was very detached, and her eyes were so vacant. She had lost five children to the orphanage. She didn't take care of them or protect them. Do you ever wonder what would become of your children without you? What if my husband and I hadn't intentionally chosen to adopt? What would have happened to my children? I think my daughter would have physically survived there, although she would have been turned out of the orphanage within a few years, at sixteen. She is clever and strong-willed and would have found a way to survive. I am not so confident about my son. I really believe he would not have made it alive to the age of twenty. But we chose life for him.

Nehemiah also chose life. He readily gave up his comfy career in the palace to care for the lives of others. That is parenting. You gave up your comfy life of sleeping in, Cheerio-less cars, and meals of your choice in quiet restaurants to care for your children. And what a full life it is. But as Grandma said in *Parenthood*, you get more out of the roller coaster of life than the predictability of the merry-go-round. And as Maxwell said, the choice you make will make you.

THE END OF THE STORY

From the time Nehemiah heard from his brother about the devastation of his people's city until the day of the wall's completion was about nine months. In the time it takes to give birth to a child, Nehemiah gave birth to renewed hope for the Israelites. The wall itself was finished in just fifty-two days and changed the course of a nation. I wonder what could be done in fifty-two weeks to change the course of a child?

When the wall was finished, the people celebrated for days, observing a holy day of rejoicing. During that time, Ezra read the law to the people and taught them how to keep it. Remember that Ezra was the man who rebuilt the temple, God's dwelling place, and then laid the foundation for his people's faith, leading them back to God.

You are called to lay the foundation for your son's or daughter's faith. You can build a strong wall to protect your child, but if you don't lay a solid foundation for what he or she believes, you will have missed your mission. Your child's heart is the dwelling place for God. Build it strong, and then protect it with your wall.

In Nehemiah 11–13, the people of Israel set up shop under Nehemiah's organized direction. After twelve years, Nehemiah returned to the palace—but not for good. Some time later Nehemiah returned to Jerusalem, like a parent on the warpath. The children had misbehaved in his absence, under the influence of none other than Mr. Tobiah, the relentless instigator. Nehemiah did not hesitate to dish out some discipline and set the Israelites straight once again—he was a faithful parent. He reported all of this in typical, direct Nehemiah fashion in the final chapter of his book.

And then, abruptly, Nehemiah closed with just one prayer: "Remember me with favor, my God" (Neh. 13:31).

In the end, Nehemiah's last concern was finding favor with God, because he was the source for all that mattered to Nehemiah. At my end, when I have crossed over that painful threshold of life, past the heart-wrenching pang as those I have loved flash before my eyes, I will be in the presence of the King. And that will be all that matters. I hope, like Nehemiah, that I will be able to say to him with confidence, *"Remember me with favor, my God."* I also hope that as I stand before him, he will remember that I, like Nehemiah, was passionate about the people he entrusted to me. I hope he will remember that I dared to parent in my world as Nehemiah dared to lead in his. I hope that as he recalls my life, he will think with favor:

> She fulfilled her purpose. She was the wall that protected her children and provided them a future. She perceived and pondered. She persevered in prayer and patience. She prepared and planned. She persevered through problems. She was the gatekeeper. She loved me. She loved her children. And her children grew in wisdom and stature and in favor with me and with others.
>
> And so did she. She was a Passionate Mom.

> *"They realized that this work had been done with the help of our God."*
>
> —Nehemiah 6:16

The Wall

The Bricks	The Mortar
Perception	Alertness Availability Attentiveness
Pondering	Self-Control Selflessness
Passion	Love Initiative
Prayer	Humility Trust
Patience	Tolerance Discipline
Preparation	Integrity Boldness Trustworthiness
Purpose	Determination
Planning	Discernment Persuasiveness
Problem Solving	Faith Courage Generosity Determination
Perseverance	

Resources

The QR code or links below will take you directly to free downloadable resources. Enjoy!

Chapter 1, page 15: TALK Cards

Get the conversation going! iMOM.com has hundreds of free printable TALK cards with questions for you and your child to share.

 Scan the QR code with your smartphone or visit http://bit.ly/imom-talk.

Chapter 4, page 73: 10 Ways to Pray for Your Child and 10 Ways to Pray for Your Teen

Pray for your child every day. Get started with one of these printables that make it easy to remember basic things you should be praying for.

 Scan the QR code with your smartphone or visit http://bit.ly/10-ways-to-pray.

Interlude, page 190: Cell Phone Contract

Clear expectations for cell phone usage will make the privilege of having a phone a safer experience for your child and less frustrating for you.

 Scan the QR code with your smartphone or visit http://bit.ly/cell-phone-contract.

Interlude, page 194: Driving Contract

Use this driving contract to talk about how you will expect your child to handle the privilege of driving.

 Scan the QR code with your smartphone or visit http://bit.ly/teen-driving-contract.

To sign up to receive iMOM's Espresso Minute daily e-mail go here:

 Scan the QR code with your smartphone or visit http://bit.ly/espresso-minute.

For more than 250 great printables and more ideas and information visit iMOM.com.

Follow Susan:

On Facebook at facebook.com/SusanMerrill
On Twitter at twitter.com/Susan_Merrill
On Pinterest at pinterest.com/Susan_Merrill
On Instagram at instagram.com/SusanMerrill

Follow iMOM:

On Facebook at facebook.com/iMOM
On Twitter at twitter.com/iMOMTweets
On Pinterest at pinterest.com/iMOMTools

Acknowledgments

MARK MERRILL

Husband, best friend

I really don't know where in the world I would be without you and the faith in Christ that we share. Our journey together amazes me. You amaze me. Your perseverance and fearlessness are my inspiration. Everything I do starts and ends with you.

NANCY JERGINS

Faithful friend and iMOM writer extraordinaire

You encouraged, provided insight, direction, and just plain propped me up when I didn't think I could do this! Your kind input was a light for me on an unfamiliar path. How can I thank God enough for all you have done for me?

MADISON ANSON

My wrangler, minute multiplier, keeper of all things iMOM, the cheerleader that I cannot live without

As usual, life got a little crazy this past year and you kept it together for me. You stepped up and managed things at iMOM with your gift of efficiency. You gave birth to Bethany in the midst of my giving birth to *The Passionate Mom* and somehow we juggled it all. God was so good to provide you for such a time as this.

LESLEY BATEMAN, KATHIE BURNS, PAIGE CODE, CHRISTIE DAVIS, JAN GRUETZMACHER, SUSAN NATIONS

The mom team

I have never thought of myself as a woman who needs a lot of encouragement until this book. My sweet group of praying women read, counseled, and provided great comfort and feedback—often on very short notice. Thank you for interrupting your life countless times to rescue me at points of uncertainty.

D. J. SNELL

Wise and kind agent

You have been so kind in your careful guidance through this process. You made every step simple and nothing I asked was ever a problem. I am deeply thankful for the graciousness with which you paved the way.

THE THOMAS NELSON TEAM

Joel Miller, Janene MacIvor, Kristen Parrish, Renee Chavez, Kristen Vasgaard, Walt Petrie, Chad Cannon, Kimberly Boyer, Brenda Smotherman

Wow, what a great group. I just don't know if it could get any better! I am beyond grateful to all of you for your experience to counterbalance my inexperience. You made me look better, read better, and feel better than I am. You did everything I expected and more.

THE WORK TEAM

Candace Mincey, Courtney Rohrdanz, Libby Watson, Jeremy Donovan, Daniel Mogg, and all the Family First staff

You are my go-to team. There is nowhere else I would rather work. Thanks for going above and beyond your Family First call of duty to help with *The Passionate Mom*.

JESSICA QUINN

Publicist and Go-to Girl

Oh girl, you are a joy! Such confidence I have in you and your tenacious, adventurous way of connecting the world.

About the Author

Photo by Ali Darvish
www.PhotoByAli.com

Susan Merrill is a hybrid of sorts. She majored in finance but loves people more than numbers. She left behind the corporate gray of banking for the colorful world of kids. She had three children and adopted two more. She is the very imperfect Merrill family manager and the director of iMOM.com. She loves to analyze life, ponder possibilities, and pray for opportunity, which makes for a very busy and messy house! She lives in Tampa, Florida, with her handsome husband—Family First founder and author Mark Merrill—and two, or depending on the day, up to five of her children ages seventeen to twenty-two. On those days, she happily forsakes all other responsibilities to run a bed and breakfast and Laundromat for college students.

Connect with Susan at:

Meet Susan's Husband
Mark Merrill

Radio Host.
The *Family Minute with Mark Merrill* is a nationally syndicated radio feature that reaches millions each weekday.

Speaker. Mark touches thousands of lives as he speaks on topics such as parenting, fatherhood, marriage, and leadership.

Author. *All Pro Dad* lays out a game plan built on seven essential fathering truths and ultra-practical insights for the questions every dad needs answered at some point.

Blogger. Social media gives Mark another way to further extend his connection to families worldwide.

President. First and foremost Mark is president and co-founder of Family First, a non-profit organization that has helped millions of moms and dads become better parents.

Connect with Mark!
Visit MarkMerrill.com.

FAMILY FIRST.